Wake Up
Your Creative Genius

Wake Up
Your Creative Genius

By Kurt Hanks & Jay Parry

CRISP.
Learning
Menlo Park, California

10 9 8 7 6
First Edition
Printed in the United States of America

Library of Congress Cataloging in Publication Data
Hanks, Kurt, 1947-
   Wake up your creative genius.

   Bibliography: p.
   1. Creative ability in technology.   2. Creative
thinking. I. Parry, Jay, 1950-   . II. Title.
T49.5.H36 1990   91-20019
ISBN 1-56052-111-2

This book was created through the joint efforts of:

Director and Designer:	Kurt Hanks
Editor:	Jay A. Parry
Art, Production, and Typesetting:	Marge Neuharth, Christine Cook, and Sheila Smith
Illustration:	Kurt Hanks
Consultants:	Larry Belliston, Dallyne Crowton, Richard Moore, Dr. Eric Stephan, Dr. William Boyd, Corrine Reed, and Ike Burke

This book is printed on recyclable paper with soy ink.

Contents

CONTENTS

The Great American Dream

Nearly everyone has the dream—making big money from their ideas.

The Great American Dream—millions are in search of it, and countless hours and dollars have been spent in pursuit of it. The dream says that everybody in the nation has the opportunity to make it big. But it's not just a fantastic daydream. The dream comes true for thousands of people every year, and this year will be no exception.

In fact, *you* may be one of the lucky ones whose dreams come true!

Every week the United States Patent and Trademark Office issues over twelve hundred beautifully prepared documents to Americans in search of that dream. Those people hope to originate or create or invent or find some idea that will bring them the pot of gold at the end of the rainbow: or they hope for fame, recognition by their peers and intellectual independence.

The Great American Dream causes millions of people to become basement tinkerers, to tote around little pads scribbled with ideas, and to spend a lot of time and energy in search of fulfillment. Those who share that dream are in good company:

- Abraham Lincoln, as a young riverboatman, invented a device for buoying vessels over shoals. He became the holder of U.S. Patent No. 6469.

- Albert Einstein once worked as a patent office clerk, and while there he got an idea for an improved refrigerator. He developed the idea and took out a patent on it.

- Mark Twain, another riverman, spent a good amount of time as a young man trying to improve certain aspects of the boats he worked on. Three of his ideas made him a considerable amount of money.

- Thomas Edison had only three weeks' formal education, and he suffered from deafness through most of his life. But through his many inventions he died a millionaire.

The Dream Comes True

Lincoln, Twain, and Edison all benefited greatly from their creative ideas, though perhaps not in the way they had expected. Many others have turned their creative ideas directly into cash. Fame and recognition have often accompanied their success. The Great American Dream

became a reality—all because of effective creativity and hard work.

Here are a few examples:

- In the late 1800s, John Pemberton invented a chemical mixture guaranteed to "whiten teeth, cleanse the mouth, harden and beautify the gums, and relieve mental and physical exhaustion." He called his formula Coca-Cola. Though it didn't bring all the benefits Pemberton claimed, it did catch on. Coke sold an average of six glasses a day in its first year. By 1980, more than 250 million servings were being sold a day. A $40 investment in the company in 1919 is now worth $6,500. All from the creative combination of coca leaves and cola nuts!

- In 1978, Dan Fylstra and a friend founded Personal Software as a project for a Harvard marketing course. Their initial investment was $500. Personal Software specialized in programs for personal computers, and Fylstra had some ideas he wanted to try out in the market. When two fellows brought him a program to help small businesses with their planning and budgeting, Fylstra saw the potential. He called the program VisiCalc and embarked on a creative marketing effort. To date, more than 200,000 copies of the program have been sold, at $250 each. The annual sales for the company are now $35 million—and climbing.

- In the mid-1970s, Bill Mitchell invented the world's first carbonated candy. The candy, called Pop Rocks, was distributed by General Foods and averaged sales of more than 150 million packages per year. Who would have thought that carbonated candy would have a future? Bill Mitchell did, and now he's working on other applications of carbonation, such as in breakfast cereal and in medicines.

- In 1905 Dr. Samuel Crumbine took time off his work on housefly eradication to go to a baseball game. The flies were proving to be tough little creatures—and it didn't help that the public seemed rather indifferent to the disease problems they posed. In the bottom of the eighth inning, the score was tied, and the home team was up at bat, with a man on third. "Sacrifice fly! Sacrifice fly!" the crowd yelled. "Swat the ball!" shouted others. "Swat the ball!"

All of a sudden, Crumbine made a connection in his mind: *Swat the fly!* He didn't even notice how the play came out.

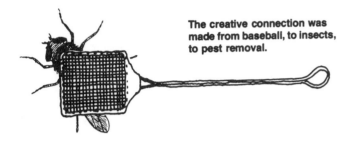

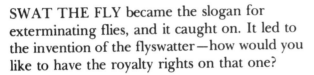

The creative connection was made from baseball, to insects, to pest removal.

SWAT THE FLY became the slogan for exterminating flies, and it caught on. It led to the invention of the flyswatter—how would you like to have the royalty rights on that one?

- During the Great Depression, the Great American Dream began to come true for James Dewar. He worked for a bakery which needed a new low-priced item to sell. Dewar came up with a small finger cake that would sell two for a nickle. "We already were selling little finger cakes during the strawberry season for shortcake," Dewar said. "The pans we baked them in sat idle except for that six-week season. So I came up with the idea of injecting little cakes with a filling." He named his little cakes Twinkies. Their producer now sells nearly a billion of them every year.

- George Nelson was a mechanic who spent forty hours a week bolting down deck plates at a San Francisco shipyard. The work was boring and slow, and Nelson began to daydream of a better way of installing the bolts. *What if an automatic gun could be developed?* he wondered. He gradually worked out the details of the idea, and within a year he had three patents to cover his stud welder. With a few friends, Nelson started

Nelson Stud Welding Corporation. A few years later he sold the company for a personal net gain of $3 million.

- Ray Kroc developed a milkshake machine that would mix five shakes at a time. One store in San Bernardino, California, a barbecue parlor owned by brothers Mac and Dick McDonald, bought eight of the mixers, and Kroc was amazed. How could any one place mix forty shakes at once? He went to investigate and was impressed by what he saw. What if there were dozens of such stores all across the country—think of the market for his mixers then!

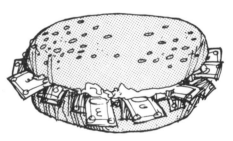

Creativity and the lowly hamburger made Ray Kroc one of the richest men in America.

He approached the McDonald brothers with his idea, but they weren't interested in further expansion. So Kroc simply bought out their name. How many billions of hamburgers has his creative marketing approach sold now? I don't dare give a number—it will be different by tomorrow!

- King Camp Gillette was tired of being a bottle-stopper salesman. Surely the Great American Dream could do better for him than that! He figured that the right invention would make the difference for him. He worked his way through the alphabet, trying to think of something lucrative to invent. But he couldn't come up with any ideas. Then one morning while he was shaving, the idea came to him: why not a presharpened, disposable blade? He developed the idea and hired a technician to produce it. He took out a patent in 1895.

It was eleven years before Gillette could scrape together the money to get his company started. And the first two years he was in business, he sold only 150 razors. But sales zoomed off the charts after that. Gillette finally retired a very rich man.

- In 1938, Chester Carlson invented the xerographic copying process. It seemed like the obvious answer to the nation's needs for reproduction of printed matter. But no one seemed to be interested. Carlson went to company after company, trying to find someone who would produce his invention. More than twenty companies turned him down. "I was met with an enthusiastic lack of interest," he said later.

But Carlson's fortunes eventually turned, and his photocopier was turned from idea into reality. It's estimated that in 1982 more than 100 billion copies were made with Carlson's xerographic process. And his company became Xerox Corporation.

Each of us can share in the Dream. It takes only three steps:

First, come up with an idea.

Second, develop it.

Third, sell it to others, so it brings a good return.

This book is a collection of concepts, principles, and techniques to enhance creativity. It contains the information you need to take you through the three steps to the Great American Dream. It will give you the most important things to think, know, and do on the way to greater creativity.

The ideas in this book are arranged in random order. The reader can select and apply them as needed. I'd suggest you mark up the book as you read. Underline the parts that help you the most. Make notes in the margin. And, most important of all, *apply* the ideas in your own life.

Creativity can make the difference in any field or situation, whether in business, the classroom, or the home. Whether your personal American Dream is to get rich, get famous, or teach your children better at home, this book can help you. It can make the difference between a bland performance and a highly successful one!

"To every man there comes in his lifetime that special moment when he is figuratively tapped on the shoulder and offered the chance to do a very special thing, unique to him and fitted to his talents. What a tragedy if that moment finds him unprepared or unqualified for the work which could be his finest hour."

Winston Churchill

A Simple Way to Start Ideas Coming

Being creative means dealing in ideas. The world runs on ideas. Good things rarely happen accidentally. Long before electric lights or television or heart surgery or even the wheel came to be, they existed as thoughts in somebody's mind.

When ideas are first formed, they are often considered to be of little importance. ("And what will you do once you're up in the air, Mr. Wright? A waste of time!") But as years pass and an idea begins to be accepted, it can change our lives. Sometimes it changes the very foundation of our society.

For instance, television has probably had a more profound effect on the way Americans think and live than anything else in the last fifty years. Yet when television was first invented by Philo T. Farnsworth, an Idaho farmboy, he had no concept of how important it would become. It was just a curiosity!

In fact, everything we deal with in our everyday lives existed first as an idea. When you snap on the light switch, remember that Thomas Edison thought of electric lights long before anybody built them. A car was an image in Henry Ford's mind long before the first Model T rolled out of the inventor's workshop.

The Source of Good Ideas

Where do good ideas come from? You're probably not a mad genius working in a laboratory, churning out miracle drugs and magic potions for a living. But that doesn't matter. Many of the extraordinary inventions we use in our world today came from quite ordinary people.

And those same ordinary people can get good ideas to improve their financial situation, their relationships with others, their circumstances at work and home, and countless other things. **Ideas can come to anyone who's willing to seek them out.**

> **"Everything that man does starts with an idea, or a succession of ideas."**
> Robert P. Crawford

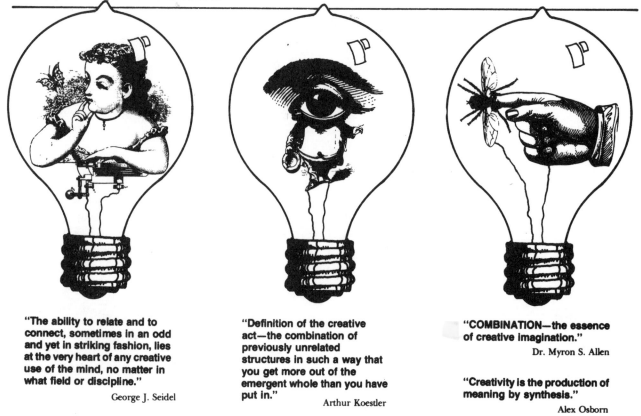

"The ability to relate and to connect, sometimes in an odd and yet in striking fashion, lies at the very heart of any creative use of the mind, no matter in what field or discipline."

George J. Seidel

"Definition of the creative act—the combination of previously unrelated structures in such a way that you get more out of the emergent whole than you have put in."

Arthur Koestler

"COMBINATION—the essence of creative imagination."

Dr. Myron S. Allen

"Creativity is the production of meaning by synthesis."

Alex Osborn

Searching Out Creative Ideas

As you seek out creative ideas to help you in your life, remember this: creation isn't making something out of nothing. Instead it's organizing existing elements into new and different wholes to produce the desired results.

Think of it in terms of the creation of new life. A sperm comes from one source, an egg from another. When the two combine, a third thing is created that's greater and more important than either of the two elements.

The same thing happens with creative ideas. An idea is picked up from one place, another idea from another place, and when the two are combined a new living idea is formed.

If we look at history, we'll see that creative ideas are rarely new. They're just old concepts combined in a new and useful way. The electric toothbrush is two old things combined: an electric motor and a toothbrush. Benjamin Franklin made the first bifocal glasses by combining two lenses in one pair of glasses. In creating the telephone, Alexander Graham Bell combined his knowledge of the human ear with his knowledge of magnetism and electricity.

Students of creativity have recognized this vital principle of combination.

"Invention is little more than new combinations of those images which have been previously gathered and deposited in the memory. Nothing can be made of nothing; those who have laid up no material can produce no combinations."

Sir Joshua Reynolds

Winning Ideas— How to Find Them

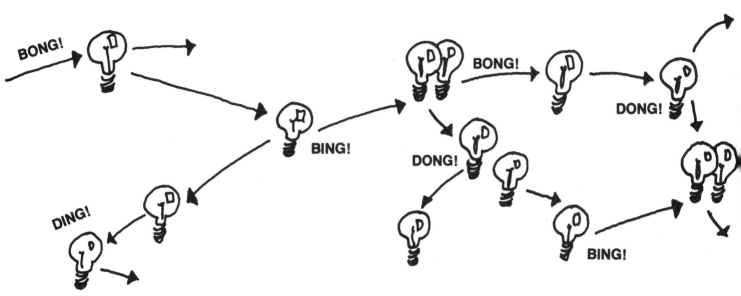

ric-o-chet (*rik-a-shay*) *n: a glancing rebound.*

In some ways, ideas are like bullets: they ricochet around. **An idea will bounce off other ideas, going from one person to the next, until it finally strikes a creative nerve.** That's when it really becomes useful. It inspires the person who's thinking about it and enables him to solve his problem.

Often the solution changes the idea so much that it's almost unrecognizable. Just like the ricocheting bullet, an idea can become mangled, but still have power to speed ahead.

Thomas Malthus's economic theories bounced around different circles for years, then hit the mind of Charles Darwin. They helped Darwin develop his theory of evolution.

Someone developed a governor for steam engines, and the idea behind the invention ricocheted back and forth until it hit the mind of a computer pioneer. From it he got the idea of feedback.

Fred Smith was trying to develop a feasible way of delivering packages overnight, nationwide, with a limited number of airplanes. He finally got the idea of central pooling his planes from the way banks pool their checks. (See page 9.)

The Nike Shoe

One morning Bill Bowerman was eating a waffle his wife had fixed him. It tasted pretty good, not

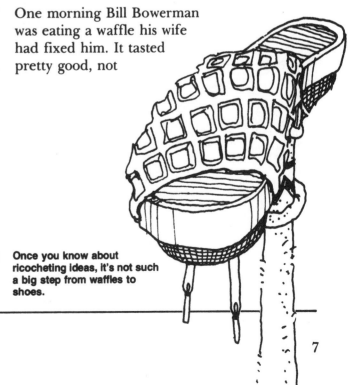

Once you know about ricocheting ideas, it's not such a big step from waffles to shoes.

As Solomon so aptly said, "Nothing under the sun is new." No idea is ever totally creative—it builds on, and from, other ideas.

7

at all like the bottom of a shoe! But as he stared at it that morning something clicked in his head. Why couldn't he take the waffle pattern and transpose it onto a good running shoe? It would cushion the foot, give good traction . . .

Bill thought about it as he chewed. It just might work. He chewed some more. Yes, it might work.

He got up from breakfast, took his wife's waffle iron—and utterly ruined it making a prototype. No matter, the idea that ricocheted into his head was a good one, and it made him enough money to buy a new waffle iron!

Ideas Bouncing Your Way

Ricocheting ideas worked for Darwin, the computer expert, Fred Smith. They worked for Bill Bowerman. They'll work for anybody. All you have to do is expose your mind to them, let them bounce off you. Eventually one will bounce in just the right place, and you'll have a winner!

One method that creates new ideas and new insights is a ricocheting process.

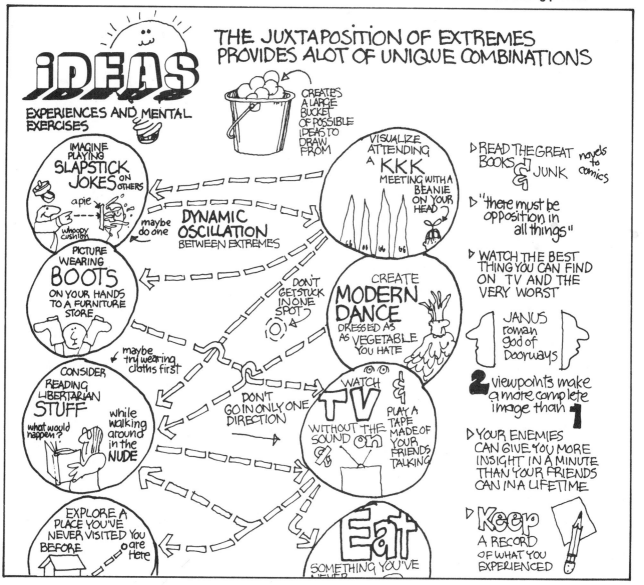

One Key to Getting Good Ideas

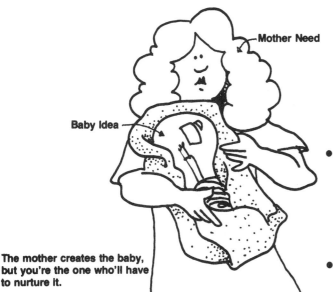

Mother Need

Baby Idea

The mother creates the baby, but you're the one who'll have to nurture it.

Need is the mother of invention. This is a universal law, one that applies to all existence. If you don't need something, you won't be very motivated to create it. The law has governed all invention, from fire to the first shoe to the compass to the computer. When there was a need, and it was perceived, someone set about filling it.

"The true creator is necessity," said Plato, "who is the mother of our invention."

Leonardo da Vinci had the same idea: "Necessity is the theme and the inventress, the eternal curb and the law of nature."

- **Henry Ford** asked his designers to come up with an eight-cylinder engine. "That's impossible," they answered. "It can't be done. An engine that powerful is only a fantasy."

  "That's fine," Ford answered. "Now go and do it anyway."

  Ford created a need—and his designers responded.

- **Jonas Salk** was concerned with the many deaths from polio. Spurred on by the need to save lives, he eventually discovered the Salk vaccine for polio, which has virtually eradicated the disease in the more advanced countries of the world.

- **A New Jersey barber** got to thinking about the laborious process of cutting hair with shears. It was slow, and it soon cramped the fingers. His need became the mother of his invention. He invented the clippers, became rich, and barbered thereafter only when he wanted to!

- **A man with a toothache** got to thinking about the pain (actually, it was all he could think about) and started to wonder if filling in the hole in the tooth would lessen the ache. Eventually he invented the gold filling.

- **A Maine farmer** had to stop his work in the hayfield to go to the house and wash the clothes for his sick wife. He'd never washed clothes before, and he was surprised at what a backbreaking job it was. Finally tiring of the whole thing, he set his mind to work—and developed the mechanical washing machine.

- **Fred Smith** noticed that some businesses had a need for overnight delivery of their packages. He formed a company that specialized in that service, called it Federal Express, and became a multimillionaire.

Here's the key to virtually all creation: Find a need and set your mind to work on it.

A Sure Way to Clog Up a Creative Mind

Sit down to a good meal. The food is exquisitely cooked. The aromas are inviting. The variety is incredible. You dig in and eat some: roast beef, broccoli in cheese sauce, green salad, potatoes with butter and sour cream, grape juice spiked with 7-Up, relishes, three varieties of breads and more roast beef. You eat and eat, and the host brings on more and more.

It doesn't take too long before you're overloaded. You gag at the thought of eating any more. And you're so uncomfortable that you don't want to get up and do anything. You don't want to think or talk. You just want to loosen your belt and belch and do nothing.

The same thing happens when we take in too much information without giving the brain a chance to process it, to digest it.

Knowing too much about a particular thing can overload the circuits and reduce creativity. Not that we should try to limit the input we get; but we *should* regulate it according to digestion.

I have a friend who's a collector of ideas. When she learns of a new idea, she grabs it and holds it tight. That's okay, I guess—except she's so overloaded with ideas that she's unable to create anything new. She once commented, "I know too much. I get so filled with great ideas that all I'm able to do is go out and collect more."

Think of the college professor who's immersed in his subject. He gets so excited about it that he tries to give it to his students all at once. They get so stuffed they can't move—and the professor wonders why they're so dense!

Ideas are important and necessary. But get too many and you'll be unable to digest them all.

"Here's a good idea. Let me add just this one more. Oh, and here's another. I might be able to use that someday. And look at this one. I'll save just this one more."

10

What You Need Besides a Good Idea

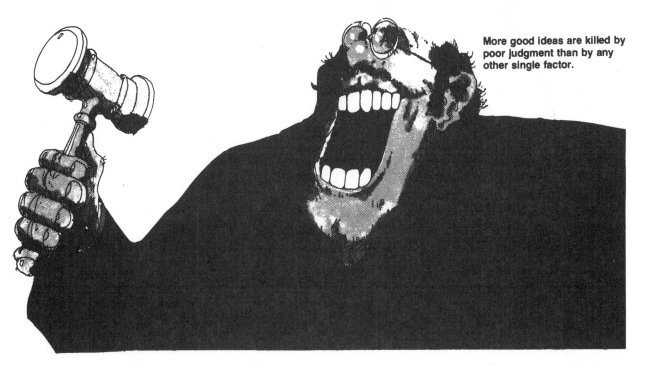

More good ideas are killed by poor judgment than by any other single factor.

"The creative process does not end with an idea; it starts with one. Creative ideas are just the first step in a long process of bringing thoughts into reality."

Alex Osborn

The time invariably comes when you need to stop collecting ideas and start judging them. All good ideas must be evaluated under the harsh light of critical thinking. The difference between just a good idea and a creative success is the ability to judge an idea effectively and then to apply it.

But the judgment shouldn't be totally cold and uncreative. **Creativity is as important in judging an idea as it is in coming up with one in the first place.**

A Bomb on Four Wheels

When Ford Motor Company came up with the idea of the Edsel, they were being creative. The designers and the executives thought they had a winner. It was a new car for a new age; it met the needs of the consumer as the company had evaluated them.

But Ford wasn't creative in that evaluation. The company looked at all the facts, but forgot to be creative in judging the creation itself. Because of that, Ford's Edsel was a sad, disastrous bomb.

Your Money Problems Are Over

When the U.S. government designers came up with the idea of the Susan B. Anthony dollar, they were being creative. The dollar would reduce the need to reprint paper money so often, since the Anthony coin would take years longer to wear out. It would work in coin machines. It was even named after a pioneer feminist, and it was issued at a time when feminism was just becoming a hot issue.

Yes, the Susan B. Anthony dollar was a creative project. It would save the government millions in printing costs.

But once they created the dollar, the designers stopped being creative. They looked at all the facts logically, rather than creatively. And therefore government officials were much surprised when the Anthony dollar was rejected by the public.

What went wrong? They never did release all the facts, but a friend's experience with the dollar gives some valuable clues:

"I'd heard of the Anthony dollar, but I'd never seen one. Then one day I went up to a soft-drink machine to quench my thirst. I pulled out a quarter and tried to drop it in the slot. It wouldn't fit. I moved to the next machine. It wouldn't fit there either. I started to curse at that blasted quarter—then I took a closer look. I had one of those stupid Anthony dollars! And I wondered how many I had given away as quarters!"

Use Your Brain to Judge Creatively

Think of your brain as containing two separate minds, with two entirely different ways of thinking. (In fact, that's almost how it is!) See one side of the brain as the idea getter and the other side as the judge. The ideal is to use both kinds of thinking. Let each one make a separate and unique contribution to your total thinking.

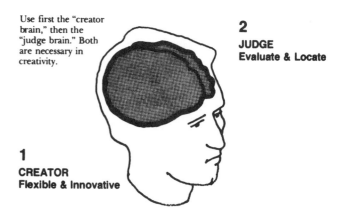

Use first the "creator brain," then the "judge brain." Both are necessary in creativity.

2
JUDGE
Evaluate & Locate

1
CREATOR
Flexible & Innovative

By using the two sides of your brain, you'll be able to be creative both in your creativity and in your judgment. In the judging, put the key emphasis not on the idea itself, but on the *results* the idea will bring.

Playful Ways
to
Get Ideas

I once visited a research center at a major university. The workers there, all highly skilled technicians, had access to the most advanced computers. We walked through room after room of the machines, and they proudly showed me what they were working on.

After I'd had the official tour, a few of us sat down to chat informally. They soon saw that I wasn't really any visiting dignitary. I was just one of the guys.

That's when they showed me what they were really interested in. It wasn't the high-level research they were working on, though, that was important to them. What they cared most about was an intricate, eighteen-hole golf course they had constructed on one of their million dollar computers.

That group at the research center confirmed an important principle: **Creative people are playful people.** They often get their best ideas just from playing around.

- Einstein liked to play games of imagination where he would ride beams of light. But the eventual result of his games was the theory of relativity. He spoke of "thought experiments."

- The telescope that Galileo invented was really just a toy for him. It wasn't until after he started using it that he saw how important it really was.

- The Chinese invented the rocket—as a toy for their little children (and their children's not-so-little dads!).

- An innovative new airplane wing design that won't allow the airplane to stall out was a direct offshoot of two designers trying to relax by flying paper airplanes around their office.

Kids are highly creative—and they're also very playful. Have we been missing an important correlation?

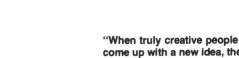

"When truly creative people come up with a new idea, they do not reject it immediately because of its flaws. They play with it, looking for strengths and sliding over weaknesses."

Dr. David Campbell

Enlarged Graffiti

David Niven tells of an afternoon when he and other creative people renewed themselves through play. He and some of Hollywood's greatest writers once spent an afternoon in New York putting together a gigantic hoax. Their plan was to get a particular four-letter word spelled out in huge letters for all to see.

Niven and his comrades worked out the details. They would forge the signature of Con Edison Company and get 438 telegrams sent out to the occupants of various offices in New York City skyscrapers with lightable windows. The telegrams would say that Con Edison was conducting a test—and would you please leave your lights on all night?

The result: the chosen four-letter word would be spelled out sixteen stories high in lights!

I don't know if Niven ever carried out the plan, but it doesn't matter. What matters is that he was playing. Through such play he was able to relax, enabling him to be refreshed and even more creative when he went back to work.

Play Is Serious Work

Being able to play is critical to a child's development. I think every parent recognizes that. But it's also critical to adult development, both physically and emotionally. It's literally impossible to create effectively, and consistently, if we're unable to let ourselves play.

- One major comedian has a complete amusement arcade in his home.

- I know a furniture designer who surrounds himself with antique toys.

- A leading management firm has a handball/racquetball court downstairs in its office building.

Why? Because creativity and play need each other. A person might be able to play without being creative, but he sure can't be creative without playing!

"Very often the effort men put into activities that seem completely useless turns out to be extremely important in ways no one could foresee. Play has always been the mainspring of culture."

Italo Calvino

Superman Syndrome

It's all right to believe you can leap tall buildings—as long as you don't jump off any. It's all right to believe you're stronger than a locomotive—as long as you don't stand in the way of one. It's all right to believe you're faster than a speeding bullet—as long as you don't jump out in front of one.

Sometimes an overabundance of pride blurs reality. A person may get working on an idea he thinks is perfect. Not because the idea is so hot, but because it's his. To him it has no faults. No weaknesses. He's certain that when he produces the idea commercially, it will sell like hotcakes. Why? Because the creator has come to think of himself as some kind of superman. It's impossible for him to create something inferior. Obviously it's the finest idea wrought by the mind of man!

I had a friend who once invented a can crusher for aluminum soda pop cans. He was super-excited about his invention. But he couldn't get anyone else excited. "They're all fools, all against me," he complained. "They don't know a good idea when they see one. Everyone has

It's rare for us to see things as they really are. But allowing the ego to obscure things even further can be very destructive.

aluminum cans they need crushed, and this will do it perfectly!"

I didn't say a word. He picked up a can and put it in his machine. I picked up a can and put it under my foot. He started up the crushing machine. I crushed down with my foot.

My foot did the job quicker than the machine. It smashed the can flatter. My foot was free and his machine was very expensive. You'd have thought the message of my actions would have been obvious. But my friend raved on. "They're so blind!"

The Super Novelist

Randy had a lifelong dream: "I'm going to write a novel," he said. "It will be fantastic. Maybe the greatest ever done."

He slaved over his book year after year, touching up here, rewriting there, refining here, adding on there. Finally it was ready. He carefully wrapped it up and sent it off to a prestigious publisher. "Once they publish this everyone is going to know my name," he said proudly.

In six weeks his manuscript came back with a form rejection. Randy sent it out again—and still again. Nobody wanted to publish it. Randy had created a piece of trash.

If you're going to make an investment in your ego, instead of your creation, at least acknowledge that that's what you're doing. Then the results won't be so crushing.

How to Strengthen Your Creative Muscle

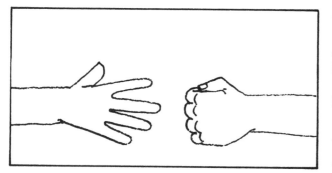

If you clench your hand all the time, it will get tired. And if you let it hang loose all the time, it will never accomplish anything. What's needed is a sequence of the two—clenched when it's time to work, loose when it's time to rest and rejuvenate.

The same thing applies to creativity. When you're tight, you're putting forth hard, concentrated effort. When you're loose, you're laid-back, having fun, maybe getting a change of scenery. **An alternation of tight and loose seems to work better than totally one or the other.**

Exercise Your Mind

Being creative is like doing isometric exercises. You push against the wall or table with all your effort. Then you rest. Both the effort and the rest are essential to the process. The combination tones your muscles. But just do one or the other and you won't get the results.

Simply working harder creatively won't bring more benefits. Just resting won't bring any. The cycle of hard, then easy, tight, then loose, is essential.

Varying from loose to tight in a continuous cycle gives the greatest creative results.

A Sure Way to Kill Creativity And How to Avoid It

"With regard to the electric light, much has been said for and against it, but I think I may say without contradiction that when the Paris Exhibition closes, electric light will close with it, and no more will be heard of it."

Erasmus Wilson
Oxford University professor, 1878

Suppose you go out to your garden to put in some corn. You fertilize the soil, using just the right kind and right amount. You loosen the hard-packed dirt with your shovel. When all danger of frost is past, you place the seeds of corn in neat rows.

As the days go by you water the seeds regularly, not letting them get too wet or too dry. Then, finally, the seeds sprout, and send up little green shoots. You take a close look. "Those don't look much like corn," you say. "And they'll never be strong enough to hold up a good ear. They don't even deserve to live." And you stomp on them, one after another, smashing them into the ground and killing them.

But what if you had been patient? What if you had decided to give those little plants another chance, to wait and see what became of them? After a few weeks the plants would have been stronger and taller, and a few weeks after that the ears would have been ready to pluck and eat.

Then you could have taken them into your kitchen, cooked them, put butter on them, and tried them out. Some of the ears might have been outstanding, some only average, some not too good. *But you wouldn't have been able to judge the corn until the ears were mature, until you had tasted them prepared the way they were meant to be prepared.*

Ideas are just like corn plants. You can't judge them at first glance; you can't decide immediately whether they deserve to live or die. Ideas are very fragile things. **They need time and care to allow them to mature before they face the critic's inevitably harsh judgment.**

Try to judge an idea too soon and you won't be able to see its full potential. Try to judge the idea too soon and you won't be able to see how it meets its potential. Ideas need to be seen in their maturity, and in the proper context. You don't judge corn by its stalk in the garden, you judge it by its taste in the kitchen.

"A new idea is delicate. It can be killed by a sneer or a yawn; it can be stabbed to death by a quip and worried to death by a frown on the right man's brow."

Charlie Brower

How to Get Big Money for Your Ideas

The ultimate creator's hell is expressed in this old Rumanian curse: "May you have a brilliant idea which you know is right and be unable to convince others."

The only time you'll get money for your creative idea is when you sell it to someone else. If you sell it well, you'll get good money. If you don't sell it at all, you'll get nothing!

Ideas don't exist in a vacuum, and neither do the products and services that come out of them. Only when other people embrace your idea will it become financially valid. You may want to sell your idea outright to someone else. Or you may want to sell distribution rights and be paid a

royalty for each sale. But no matter what your approach, other people will need to get involved in:

    manufacturing
    distributing
    selling
    marketing

Moving from creation to selling requires a change in emphasis. The creator is the key in the first step of the process. He's uninhibited in how he works—and he can create anything he likes.

But when the time for marketing comes, the problem changes. The marketer becomes the key person. His application must be practical and

---

NOTE: If you chose answer A on the test above, maybe you'd better find something else to do with your life!

appealing to the public, or it will never get off the ground. And often the marketer must spend more time and money than the creator did!

Marketing

According to a recent study, 75 percent of the money many companies spent on new product research, development, and marketing was totally wasted. The resulting products never made a profit. Industry and business in the U.S. spends $25 *billion* a year researching and developing new products. But developing ideas and profiting from them are two different things.

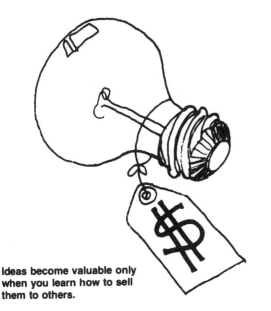

Ideas become valuable only when you learn how to sell them to others.

A common mistake is for creative people to originate an idea without thoroughly considering the marketing of the resulting product. Will people want to buy the new product? Are they willing to pay the required cost? Is the item really needed? Are there established channels of distribution for the sale of the item?

Decisions about selling the idea should be made right up front, along with the creative decisions. When Michael Faraday invented the electric motor, he took it to the Prime Minister of Great Britain, William Gladstone, for backing. When Gladstone looked at the crude prototype, which

was little more than a wire revolving around a magnet, he wasn't much impressed.

"What good is that?" he asked.

Faraday was ready with his answer. "Someday you will be able to tax it," he said.

His point was made, and Gladstone offered the support Faraday needed. All because Faraday knew how to sell his idea to someone else.

A Few Key Points

As you seek to market your creations, keep these points in mind:

First, one person rarely has the talent to both create and market an idea. You'll almost certainly need to get the help of someone else.

Second, marketing usually involves a change in point of view. Your creation will mean different things to you than it will to anyone else. When Faraday showed his motor to Gladstone, he could easily have told Gladstone of his great visions of the future of the motor. Instead, he approached it from Gladstone's point of view—and accomplished his goal.

If you can come up with a product or idea that gives people what they want, from their point of view, you'll be much more successful in selling it. Ralph Waldo Emerson said:

"If a man write a better book, preach a better sermon or make a better mouse-trap than his neighbour, tho he build his house in the woods, the world will make a beaten path to his door."

Third, remember it's *who* you know that counts. Personal contact with the marketer or buyer of your idea is critical. And if you can get someone to refer you to someone else, so much the better. As Alden Perkes put it, "Knowing and convincing the right kind of people opens the right kind of doors."

Fourth, be ready to answer the important questions about your creation. What will the cost per unit be? What is the expected product life? What market segment do you anticipate the idea will appeal to?

Fifth, look and act professional. I've seen far too many good ideas bomb because of poor presentation. You'll have to look and act as if you know what you're doing.

Before his idea will have any financial value, the creator must become a salesman. He's got to sell both himself and his creation. And that means he's got to go out and meet people and make things happen. As Stewart Britt said (and this applies to selling your ideas), "Doing business without advertising is like winking at a girl in the dark. You know what you are doing, but nobody else does."

The economic value is not decided by yourself but by the people who buy your idea. What they pay is what it is worth.

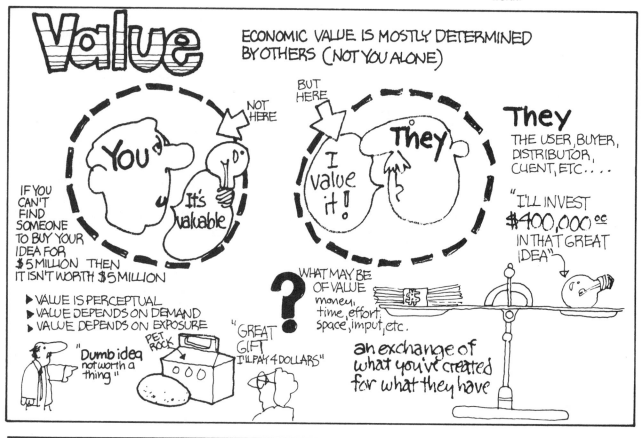

How to Make Ideas Valuable

"Ideas are cheap and abundant; what is of value is the effective placement of those ideas into situations that develop into action."

Peter Drucker

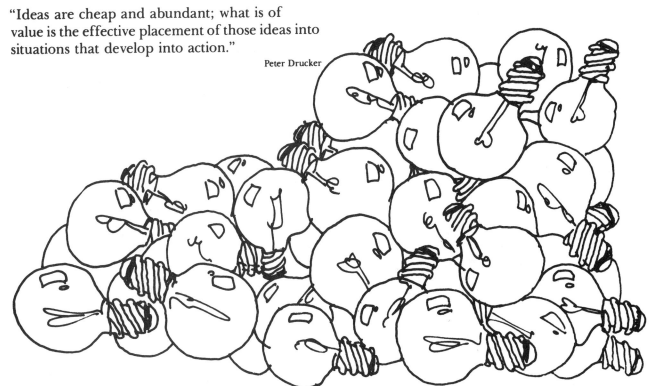

I love ideas. It's easy for me to sit down and come up with a good batch of creative ideas in very short order.

But there's a big difference between getting ideas and doing something with them. At one point, several years ago, I realized that I was drowning under the accumulation of great ideas that weren't doing me a bit of good. They were inert, lacking life, and they may as well have not existed.

An idea all by itself is nice enough. But it doesn't mean much unless it's attached to people and things. I decided I'd better change my approach—I would spend my creative energy in the selection and application of just a few ideas. If I didn't see an application to a particular idea, I'd discard it and go on to another one that I could apply.

Place Ideas Properly to Produce Results

That approach has made all the difference. **Ideas by themselves are utterly useless.** The value comes when you apply them. It's the *results* ideas bring that makes them valuable.

> "Ideas are useless unless used. The proof of their value is in their implementation. Until then, they are in limbo. . . .
>
> "Many of the people with the ideas have the peculiar notion that their jobs are finished when they suggest them; that it is up to somebody else to work out the dirty details and then implement the proposals. Since business is a 'get-things-done' institution, creativity without action-oriented follow-through is a barren form of behavior."
>
> Theodore Leavitt
> *INC.*, Feb. 1981, p. 96

Ideas are the stuff that creativity is made of. But they have to be used to be worthwhile.

Here Lies A Good Idea

How to Make Your Ideas Succeed

A golf ball that can be steered in mid flight would ruin the game.

The Incomplete Book of Failures (Stephen Pile, New York: E.P. Dutton, 1979) has an entry about the world's "most unsuccessful inventor." The man, named Arthur Pedrick, patented 162 inventions between 1962 and 1977 (and probably more since)—and not a one of them was ever produced commercially.

His inventions included a bicycle "with amphibious capacity," a car attachment that would enable a person to drive the car from the back seat, and a golf ball that could be steered in flight.

One of Pedrick's greatest ideas was a method of irrigating the world's deserts by sending giant snowballs from the polar regions.

No one can doubt that Arthur Pedrick is highly creative. But there's a reason why his inventions fail: **An idea can only succeed when the self-interest of the creator and the self-interest of the user don't conflict.**

A conflict between the creator and the user is a sure way to kill an idea.

"This is a fantastic idea—it's my baby!"

"But it doesn't do what I need or want!"

Sphere of influence

The creator is often blind to what the user or buyer will see in his idea.

The buyer and user will pay only for those things he or she wants.

Sphere of influence

The creator may have tremendous creative energies. But he can't use them in a vacuum.

For example, if you could steer a golf ball in mid flight, it would take all the fun out of the game. Besides, it's against the rules! And why would anyone ever want to steer a car from the back seat?

If the creation doesn't meet the needs of both the creator and the user, it will fail every time.

Edison Learns a Lesson From Failure

Thomas Edison learned this principle the hard way. While he was still a young man, he invented a vote-counting machine, designed to be used in legislative chambers. The legislator could sit at his desk, flip a switch on the machine, and record his vote as "yea" or "nay." The machine would eliminate the processes of marking ballots and counting up the votes. It would be a real time and energy saver.

Edison was certain the machine would be a real winner. He got a patent on it and headed for Washington. There he met with the Chairman of the Congressional Committees.

"It's a wonderful idea," the chairman said. "You're obviously a very ingenious young man."

Edison beamed.

"But we can't use it," the chairman continued.

"What? Why?" Edison responded.

"Young man, Congress is limited by its rules and regulations. Filibustering and delay in the tabulation of votes are often the only means we have for defeating bad or improper legislation."

Edison was stunned. His invention was a good one—and he knew the chairman knew it. *But it didn't meet the need.* Said Edison, "There and then I made a vow that I would never invent anything which was not wanted."

His vow is a good one for all of us. It's crucial that we avoid conflicting self-interest. Success will come only when we give other people what they really want, not what we want them to want.

The easiest way to succeed as a creator is to meet the needs of people. And one good way to meet their needs is to give them the rewards they want—and help them avoid the punishments they don't want.

Many people desire:

to avoid effort
to save time
to make a lot of money
to achieve comfort
to be healthy
to be popular
to enjoy pleasure
to be clean
to be in control
to be praised
to be smart
to be in style
to gratify curiosity
to satisfy an appetite
to attract the opposite sex
to be a unique individual
to emulate desired models
to take advantage of opportunities
to be important
to have possessions
to have a good reputation
to avoid trouble
to feel blameless
to be competent
to know why
to be safe
to eliminate worry
to be in a desired group
to be happy

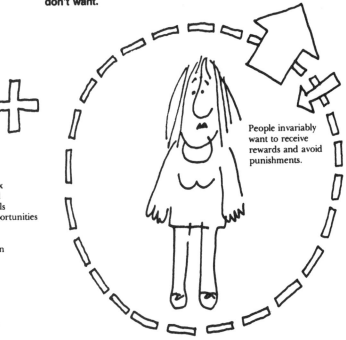

People invariably want to receive rewards and avoid punishments.

Most people want to avoid:

strenuous effort
losing time
losing money
discomfort
ill health
being neglected
pain
being dirty
being controlled
criticism
being stupid
being out of style
boredom
being unable to satisfy an appetite
repelling the opposite sex
being a boring person
failing to emulate models
failing to take advantage of opportunities
failing to be important
losing possessions
losing reputation
trouble
guilt
incompetence
failing to understand
danger
worry
being left out
unhappiness

"There and then I made a vow that I would never invent anything which was not wanted."

Thomas Alva Edison

Projection

"Ideas are vantage points which provide new perspectives."

In solving creative problems, it often helps to change point of view. Try to put yourself in another position. There's an old proverb that says, "What a tiger eats becomes a tiger." If you want to solve a problem, first become part of the problem. Let "the tiger eat you." When you let yourself assume a new point of view, you'll see things in a whole new light.

"An important key to creative success is looking at things from the right perspective."

Tom Comell

Whenever you're faced with a difficult creative problem, project yourself to the end. Projection involves seeing things from the point of view of the completed project. See the means you use to get to the end, the tool you use, and the results you obtain. By using this approach you'll be able to have a new perspective, and new perspective can often help you see solutions you were unable to see before.

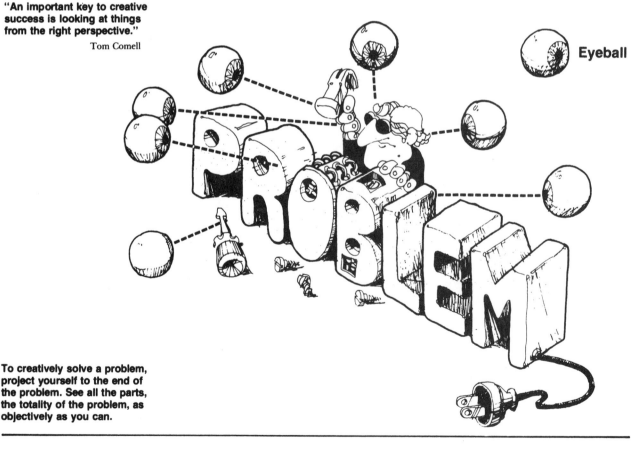

Eyeball

To creatively solve a problem, project yourself to the end of the problem. See all the parts, the totality of the problem, as objectively as you can.

Getting More from Your Mind

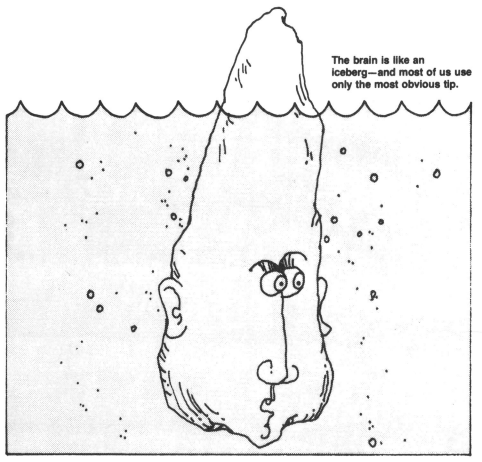

The brain is like an iceberg—and most of us use only the most obvious tip.

Most people use only 10 percent of their total brain power. Some 90 percent remains forever untouched. Part of the problem is our laziness. It's easy to let someone else do our creative thinking for us. At their jobs, a lot of people do only what they're told. At home we let television babysit us, stealing from us opportunities to think, imagine, dream, invent, create. We participate in mindless, trivial conversation.

Exercise Your Brain

Is it any wonder that so many people don't know how to use their brains!

Put your arm in a cast and secure it tightly against your chest, leaving it that way for three months. What will happen? In addition to ugly skin, you won't be able to use the arm after you remove the cast. The muscles will atrophy, will weaken from disuse, leaving you with an arm too weak to use.

The human mind is like a muscle. When we don't use it, we weaken its ability to function. It suffers a form of mental atrophy. To develop the ability to produce good ideas, you have to exercise your brain. You become a good golfer by understanding the game of golf and then practicing diligently. It's the same way with the mind. We have to understand the techniques of creativity, and then practice them.

"Few people think more than two or three times a year; I have made an international reputation for myself by thinking once or twice a week."

George Bernard Shaw

The beginning of creativity is committing ourselves to getting started. **Then, once we've decided to get going, we need to start practicing.** Take the ideas in this book and put them to use. Try one. Then try another. Gradually we'll be using that 10 percent of our brains more and more effectively. And maybe we'll even be able to increase the *percentage* of the brain we use.

Thinking is enjoyable, but it takes time. The creator must be willing to expend some hard mental work. He must be willing to expect more of himself—more new ideas, more creative solutions, more dreams becoming reality. It's easy to let the mind be a sponge, to soak up the situations and experiences that come from day to day. But, even though it's harder, it's much more important that the mind be thought of as a muscle, flexing and strengthening and growing.

A Challenge

Stop now, go to your desk, and get a very frightening thing—at least, it's frightening to some people. Pick up a blank sheet of paper. Use it to start exercising your mental muscles. List some problems confronting you that require creative solutions. Then think creatively and come up with some ideas that might solve these problems. They may not be the perfect answers, but you have to start somewhere.

The key to your own creative future is sitting right between your ears. Use it!

3

"Iron rusts from disuse; water loses its purity from stagnation and in cold weather becomes frozen; even so does inaction sap the vigors of the mind."

Leonardo da Vinci

"The mind is not a vessel to be filled but a fire to be kindled."

Plutarch

How we see ourselves (our self-image) is proportional to our creative output.

The Outside Advantage

WHAT BIRD?

When we get too close to a problem we often can't see what it's all about.

Sometimes an outsider can help in creativity—even though the outsider is inexperienced in the area involved.

Looking Too Long to See Clearly

I used to like to paint pictures. Sometimes I'd work for hours on a painting and just couldn't get it right. Something was wrong, but I couldn't really identify what it was.

Along would come my wife. She'd see the problem immediately. "Why is the sky this color over here?" she'd ask. Or, "Don't you think that barn is disproportional?" Or, "Who ever saw grass like that?"

Here I'd worked and sweated and labored for hours and my wife put her finger on the problem in an instant. She couldn't paint. But she did have eyes. And she was an outsider, someone not intimately involved with the work at hand.

Those who are too close to the problem can't see it clearly....

Sometimes you can solve problems by removing yourself from them.

But those who are removed from the problem can often see it in perspective.

The outside person is often the one who comes up with the solution.

Sometimes we get too close to a problem to see the solution. Sometimes we get so close that we don't even know there's a problem in the first place.

The longer you work with a problem the more it becomes a part of you. And the more it becomes a part of you the harder it is to see the problem objectively.

This lack of objectivity can get so bad that the only way to see clearly is to get an outsider to take a look.

Free to See Clearly

You'd think that most of the great developments of the world came through skilled people, trained in their field. But that's just not the case. The trained people are often too close to the problem to see what the real solution is.

- Kodachrome film was developed by a musician.
- The ballpoint pen was invented by a sculptor.
- The pneumatic tire was developed by a veterinarian.
- The long-playing record was developed by a television engineer.
- The automatic telephone was developed by an undertaker.
- The parking meter was invented by a journalist.
- Louis Pasteur was not an M.D.
- The Wright brothers were bike mechanics, not aeronautical engineers.
- Albert Einstein was a mathematician, not a physicist.

"We don't know who first discovered water, but we can be sure it wasn't a fish."

Howard Gossage

How to Protect Your Ideas

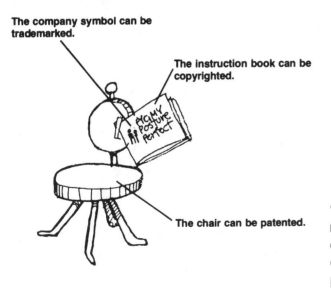

One of the worst things that could ever happen is if someone else stole your idea. Prevent that by locking it up well!

If you think your idea has financial merit, or if you feel it's important that you are recognized as the originator of the idea, you may want to seek legal protection. There are several kinds of legal protection of ideas—but all apply only to the idea's application. An idea all by itself can't be protected.

So the idea has to be developed. The tune in your head has to be put onto paper. The invention has to be taken to the point of working drawings. The story has to be written. Only then will you be ready to seek the kinds of protection the government can give.

That protection falls into three basic categories: patent, copyright, and trademark.

The Pygmy Posture Perfect

Suppose, for instance, that you develop a new kind of chair especially for midgets. You decide to call it Pygmy Posture Perfect. The chair is unique enough that you seek a patent to cover it—and the patent is granted. To make the chair more marketable, you write a little booklet to be sold with it. That booklet is copyrighted, so no one else can legally rip you off. Then, since you have such a red-hot name for the chair, you decide to get trademark protection for the name "Pygmy Posture Perfect."

The company symbol can be trademarked.

The instruction book can be copyrighted.

The chair can be patented.

"I've been involved in some legal trouble with my ideas. I've learned you should keep track of everything you do. Get all the protection you can get. And have a knowledge of what that protection can do and can't do for you."

David Meeker

These three kinds of protection really cover about any situation you might run across. Let me explain more about how each one works.

Patents

- Grants issued by the U.S. government giving you the exclusive right to make, use, and sell your invention. Of course, if you wish to sell or give away that right, you may.

- Good for 17 years—unless the invention dealt only with the visual appearance of the product. Then the patent may be good for 3½, 7, or 14 years.

- Not obtainable if the product has been on the market for more than one year, or has been described in publication more than one year earlier.

- Takes an average of 19 months to obtain—often longer. Costs up to $1500—often more.

- Not obtainable if the invention doesn't differ in some significant way from other items already under patent. To find what's under patent, a patent search must be conducted. A patent agent or patent attorney can conduct the search—it's complicated—or you can do it yourself. Contact your local public or university library to find out where the nearest patent catalog is located.

- Patent agents and patent attorneys are usually needed to file an application—the application requires a good deal of complicated legalese. Once the application is filed, the Patent and Trademark Office issues a patent pending status, which puts your invention in their files until a patent is actually issued.

- A listing of patent agents and patent attorneys can be obtained by writing for the booklet, *Attorneys and Agents Registered to Practice before United States Patent Office*. Write to Superintendent of Documents, U.S. Government Printing Office, Washington, D.C. At this writing, there was a $1 mailing fee.

You'll need to do a patent search to find out if your idea has already been done.

Patents give only broad coverage, and it's often possible for the competition to design around the patent.

Your patent

The competition

Trademarks

- These protect the name or symbol connected with your business.

- To receive trademark protection, your mark or name must differ in some significant way from those already registered, as well as from those already in use but not registered.

- A trademark search may be conducted to make sure your mark is unique. A patent attorney or agent can assist you in this search.

- Trademarks are different from trade names—the actual name of the business. Instead they represent brand names or symbols.

- A brand name is automatically protected by law—but registration with the trademark office greatly simplifies matters if someone infringes on your trademark and the case goes to court.

- Trademarks can be obtained to identify a company's unique services, as well as goods.

- Trademark registration is for 20 years. It can then be renewed for 25 year terms, indefinitely.

- Application forms can be obtained from the Commissioner of Patents and Trademarks, Washington, D.C. 20231. Note whether your application will be filed in the name of an individual, a partnership or company, or a corporation.

- At present there is a $35 fee for filing a trademark.

Copyrights

- Copyrights cover the *form* an idea is expressed in. The law will not copyright an idea in itself.

- Copyrights cover everything from books to brochures, and advertisements to movies, records, pictures, graphic works, and sculpture.

- Copyrights are granted automatically when a work is created. The copyright should be protected by making an official application, however.

- Application forms may be obtained from the Copyright Office, Library of Congress, Washington, D.C. 20559.

- The completed application form must be sent in with two copies or photos of the work and a $10 fee.

- Under the new law, your copyright will be good for your lifetime plus an additional 50 years.

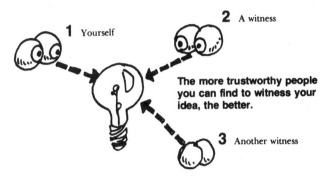

The more trustworthy people you can find to witness your idea, the better.

Get a Witness

Once you have determined that you have a marketable idea and that you want to invest the time and money to protect it, get a trustworthy friend to sign his name as a witness on a dated drawing or description of the invention. Also keep careful records of the steps you take, along with the date of each. At a later time you might have to prove when you first conceived the idea, when you made a written description or drawing, and when you built and tested the item. To prove such facts to the satisfaction of the Patent and Trademark Office or a United States court, your own word must be supported by that of another person who has knowledge of the facts from firsthand observation. Also keep any correspondence about the invention and sales slips of material purchased for it, in case they are needed to help substantiate facts and dates at a later time.

You may also want to have a notary public witness your signature, as well as your friend's. Additional protection can be obtained by sending a registered letter to yourself, which will make the date a matter of official post office record.

Make a Disclosure Statement

To help you establish evidence of the date of conception of your idea, you can file a disclosure statement with the Patent and Trademark Office. Any paper disclosing an invention and signed by the inventor or inventors is acceptable. It will be retained for two years and will then be destroyed, unless it is referred to in a related patent application filed within two years.

A disclosure document doesn't diminish the value of conventional witnessed and notarized records as evidence of conception of an idea, but it does provide a creditable form of evidence. The disclosure statement also doesn't take the place of an application for patent.

The disclosure document must take the form of written matter or drawings on paper or other thin, flexible material, such as linen or plastic drafting material, having dimensions or being folded to dimensions not to exceed 8½ by 13 inches. Photographs are also acceptable. Each page should be numbered. Text and drawings should be sufficiently dark to permit reproduction with commonly used office copying machines.

In addition to the fee (discussed below), the disclosure document must be accompanied by a stamped, self-addressed envelope and a separate paper in duplicate, signed by the inventor, stating that he is the inventor and requesting that the material be received for processing under the Disclosure Document Program. The papers will be stamped by the Patent Office with an identifying number and date of receipt, and the duplicate will be returned in the self-addressed envelope together with a warning notice indicating that the disclosure document may be relied upon only as evidence and that a patent application should be filed if patent protection is desired.

The creator's patent request may take the following form:

"The undersigned, being the inventor of the disclosed invention, requests that the enclosed papers be accepted under the Disclosure Document Program, and that they be preserved for a period of two years."

A fee of $10 is charged for this service. Payment must accompany the disclosure document when it is submitted to the Patent Office. A check or money order must be made payable to "Commissioner of Patents." Mail with the disclosure document to "Commission of Patents, Washington, D.C. 20231."

The two-year retention period should not be considered to be a "grace period," during which the inventor can wait to file his patent application without possible loss of benefits. If a problem develops and you must establish priority of invention, in addition to a disclosure document you'll need to establish diligence in completing the invention or in filing the patent application subsequent to the filing of the disclosure document.

One other caution: any public use or sale of the invention in the United States, or publication of the invention anywhere in the world, more than one year prior to filing the patent application will prohibit the government from granting the patent.

If you aren't familiar with what is considered to be "diligence in completing the invention" or "reduction to practice" under the patent law, or if you have other questions about patent matters, consult an attorney or agent registered to practice before the Patent Office. Patent attorneys and agents may be found in the telephone directories of most major cities.

Jumping the Creativity Gap

You can take a lot of time finding a creative solution—or you can save a lot of time and energy taking a creative leap.

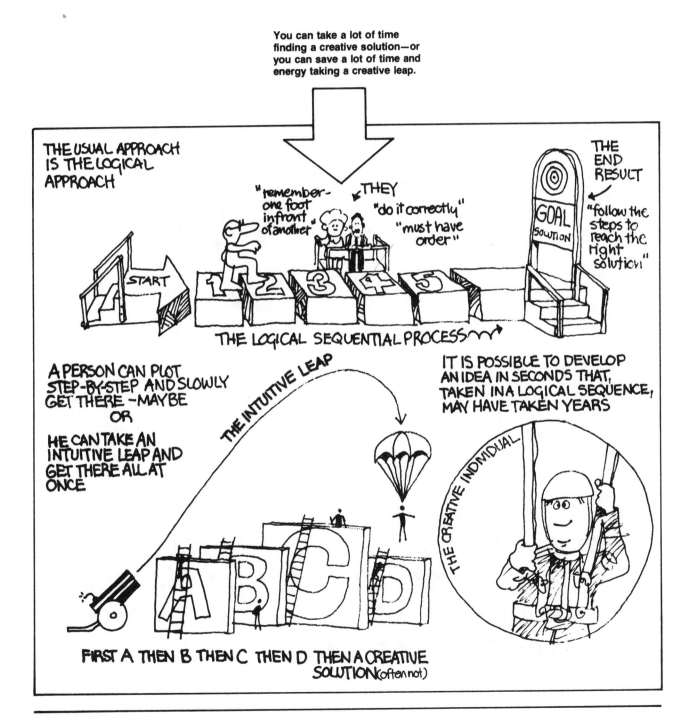

Follow a line of logic and it will take you only so far. But take the intuitive leap and suddenly you're working with a whole new creative idea.

Jumping to the Right Conclusion

The theory of relativity isn't logical at all—until Einstein makes an intuitive leap and explains it!

It didn't make a bit of sense at the time to think that the earth *wasn't* the center of the universe—until Copernicus took an intuitive leap and explained it!

Logic would never take a person from a hard crank plus a camera to motion pictures—but Edison reached that point with his intuitive leap!

The intuitive leap comes when a person makes a sudden jump to the solution of a problem without taking the intervening steps.

If A equals B and B equals C and C equals D, then A equals D. That's all logical.

But when a person takes the intuitive leap, he's able to jump from A to D in one step. It's a great creative approach!

Kroc's Leap

Ray Kroc took the intuitive leap when he bought McDonald's in 1960. His lawyer told him he was making a bad deal, paying $2.7 million for a couple of hamburger stands with a great name. Kroc says, "I closed my office door, cussed up and down, threw things out of the window, called my

lawyer back, and said: 'Take it!' I felt in my funny bone it was a sure thing."

Kroc's leap paid off. Sales in the hamburger chain are now in the billions annually.

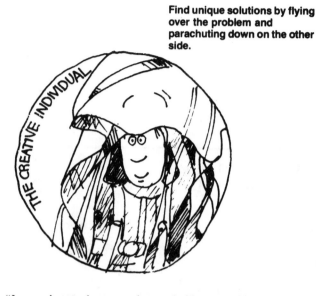

Find unique solutions by flying over the problem and parachuting down on the other side.

THE CREATIVE INDIVIDUAL

"It may have taken months, probably years, if I had continued on the route I had committed myself to. But the final solution was there in a flash. It came while I was eating breakfast."

John E. Williams

"There are ways of doing things better that don't seem logical. In speedreading, things switch around at the high speeds. Instead of going word by word, sentence by sentence, paragraph by paragraph, an entire page can be absorbed at once."

Larry Belliston

"If a man does not keep pace with his companions, perhaps it is because he hears a different drummer. Let him step to the music which he hears, however measured or far away."

Henry David Thoreau

Thinking Traps That Kill Creativity

"Nature has no watertight compartments. Every phenomenon affects and is affected by every other phenomenon."

Theodore Cook

There are many ways to be creative. One of the best is through combination—we take ideas from one source, combine them with ideas from another source and come up with a great new idea.

But at the same time, we erect walls around ourselves and the categories we think in. Professor Jackson is into literature—and he isn't interested in any ideas in mathematics. Arnie Wilkes is a research chemist—and he could care less about sociology.

The result: neither Jackson nor Wilkes is able to be as creative as he'd like. **Since combination is often the essence of creative ideas, the walls we construct restrict the associations we can make. And we end up with fewer combinations.**

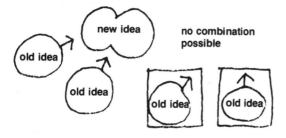

Think about most universities. The different disciplines are divided into separated compartments. They're made airtight. If you're not a member of that group, you won't be able to get in. If you are a member, you won't be able to get out.

The Painful Result of Compartments

What does that do to creativity? The people in the compartments can't see what's beyond their walls. The answer to their problems may be right next door, but they can't see it. They've been limited in the ideas they have exposure to, and they're therefore limited in the *new* ideas they can come up with.

Compartments are a human invention. They're not absolute. For example, a tree will be seen differently by different people. An artist will see one thing and a biologist another. A lumberman will see one thing, a camper another, a bird still another.

Which is right? All of them! A tree is really the combination of perceptions everyone has, and more besides. But by putting it into compartments, the viewer will be limited in what he can do with the tree.

> "A keen observer once said of Einstein that part of his genius was his inability to understand the obvious."
>
> Henry Eyring

Creative Hype

A movie producer once walked into my office, wanting to work on a project with me. He spent a lot of effort on his image—he did all he could to convince me he was hot stuff. Talk, talk, talk, and all about himself.

The conclusion of his sales pitch: *"I don't mind telling you, I'm creative as hell!"*

We decided to give him a try. At least we'd look at his stuff. Finally he brought it in. Terrible! It was some of the worst work I've ever seen.

Some people spend all of their time and effort (and sometimes money) trying to look the part of the creative person. There's only one problem: people who are truly creative work at creating not hyping. Their work will speak for itself.

And if a person isn't creative, all his hype won't work for very long. You can fool some of the people some of the time, but you can't fool all of the people all of the time.

Creative Hype

Think about the creative people you know. They're not worried about how they look, about the image they portray. They're not trying to look the part. All they're trying to do is create.

- Go into the inventor's workshop. Is he wearing a three-piece suit? Are vials and test tubes neatly stacked in holders on the shelf? Probably not. His hair is probably messed up. His workbench

Which is more important—to LOOK creative or to BE creative?

is a mess. You wonder how he can ever find what he's working on. Yet the man's a genius.

- Look at the professor who gives such brilliant lectures. One day he wears his sneakers with his suit, by mistake. Another day he doesn't pay attention and puts on one white sock and one black one.

- The fashion designer, who makes such nice clothes for all the rich folks—what does she look like? She wears a tacky blazer jacket. Even has a closet full of them. Not because she doesn't know better, but just because she doesn't care. She doesn't want to waste time looking the part.

In the effort to be creative, there are two ways we can spend our time:

1. Trying to look creative. (**Look it!**)

2. Being creative. (**Be it!**)

Ultimately, which is more important?

One Reason Your Good Ideas May Fail

A creator may have the best idea in the world. It may revolutionize our lifestyles. It may completely renew our way of thinking. But if the idea comes out at the wrong time or wrong place, it won't succeed. **An idea is doomed to failure if its placement is wrong.**

An idea can have faulty placement in a variety of ways:

It comes out at the wrong time.
It's produced in the wrong culture.
The amount is wrong.
The style is wrong.
The positioning is wrong.

An idea is impossible to isolate from its context. A good idea poorly placed will fail almost every time. A good idea that's well-placed will succeed.

"It's just as sure a recipe for failure to have the right idea fifty years too soon as five years too late."

J. R. Platt

Even the best idea must be put in the right context.

Cooked Goose

Once upon a time a wizard gave me a very young goose. This was a very special goose. Its feathers were pure white, white as freshly fallen snow. Its neck curved gracefully up to a perfectly formed head.

But the beauty of the goose wasn't the best part. Because when this goose matured, it would be able to lay *golden eggs*.

At first I couldn't believe that a goose could do such a magical thing. Then the wizard showed me the eggs laid by my goose's mother: they were solid gold. Each one was worth a fortune.

"Nine out of ten of the eggs your goose lays will be golden. The tenth will give you a new gosling, which will grow up and lay more golden eggs," the wizard explained.

My wife and I were delighted. Each day we'd go out into our backyard and feed our goose some special goose food. We'd feed it scraps from our table—but only if they were fresh, and only if they hadn't gotten dirty. Only the best for our goose! We wanted it to grow up and lay golden eggs.

Then we fell on hard times. I lost my job. My wife couldn't find work. We went on welfare. We started using food stamps. Somehow we couldn't make ends meet. No longer could we afford expensive goose food for our goose; it had to get by on ordinary goose grain.

One snowy night my wife sat down to still another meal of boring soup and a strange look came into her eyes. "Do you realize it's been months since we had fresh meat?" she asked.

I nodded. I realized it all too well.

"Do you know that grain-fed goose is some of the finest, most tender meat there is on this planet?"

I looked up. I knew what she was thinking. She was really going to cook my goose!

"But—but what about the golden eggs?" I asked.

"Surely you don't really believe all that nonsense!" my wife exclaimed. She picked up her carving knife and headed for the door.

"But what if it's true?" I shouted after her.

She never did answer.

That cooked goose sure tasted good.

A lot of fairy tales can be applied to how things really work. If you're ever stuck creatively, it might help to take a look at some of the fairy tales you know.

A Sure-Fire Creative Technique

Someone else invented the vacuum cleaner before Hubert Booth did. There was only one problem: it didn't work.

Booth saw a demonstration of the vacuum at a London music hall in 1901. The inventor turned on his machine—and blew dirt all over the audience. After the demonstration Booth decided to have a word with the inventor. "You don't quite have it," Booth said. *It should suck, not blow."*

The inventor was outraged. "It works great. Gets rid of the dirt completely. And sucking isn't possible."

Booth disagreed. He built his own vacuum cleaner, but he did a little something extra. He made his device suck, not blow. His invention now cleans the floors of the world.

Successful creative solutions are often an extra modification or adaptation to an existing thing. Instead of looking for something completely new, the creator takes a look at things that are already around, to see how he can adapt them to his needs.

- **John Deere** became famous when he took the iron plow and made a little modification: he made it with steel. America's farmlands haven't been the same since.

- **Orville and Wilbur Wright** saw others trying to invent the airplane and failing. The Wright brothers did something extra—they attached movable flaps to the wings—and became successful.

- **Phillip Reis** invented the telephone before Alexander Graham Bell did. But it would send only singing, not speaking. Bell came along and adapted it—using continuous rather than interrupted current—and drew the applause of the world.

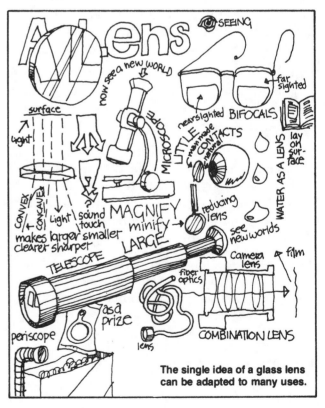

The single idea of a glass lens can be adapted to many uses.

How to Turn Mistakes into Opportunities

Oftentimes the truly creative solution to a problem isn't where we expect it to be. We can look and look in a particular place for an answer. Then, suddenly, we'll find the answer somewhere else.

This "method" of creatively finding answers is called *serendipity*. **It's serendipity when we look at one thing and then, by a lucky accident, see another.**

- **Sir Alexander Fleming** was doing an experiment with bacteria in a Petri dish. During the night some mold blew through his window into the dish. The bacteria around the mold all died. Fleming discovered penicillin—through a lucky accident!

- **Two Swedish surgeons** were disturbed to see a bottle of dextran (used in blood transfusions) fall into a sink and break. Then they were surprised: the dextran absorbed the water in the sink. With a little thought, they were able to develop a powder from the dextran that heals open, oozing wounds like magic.

- **Charles Goodyear** was trying to make rubber into something useful. But the substance changed consistency so much, the task was nearly impossible. On hot days it was soft and sticky; on cold days it was hard and brittle. One day while he was working with it, he accidentally spilled some on his stove—and discovered the process of vulcanization.

When opportunity knocks, will anybody be home?

- **Constantine Fahlberg** was working with a new combination of chemicals in 1879 and rubbed an itching lip without washing his hands. The sweet substance he tasted when he licked his lips became a substitute for sugar, saccharin.

- **W.C. Roentgen** in 1895 was experimenting with cathode rays—and just happened to have a sheet of paper covered with barium platinocyanide nearby. When he shined his rays, he noticed that the paper glowed. It was a happy accident. He had discovered the existence of X-rays.

- **Hans Christian Oersted** in 1819 was demonstrating some of the characteristics of electricity to students. When he passed an electric current through a wire, he saw the needle jerk on a compass that just happened to be nearby. Through serendipity, Oersted discovered electromagnetism.

- **A chemist** found through an experiment some stuff in a test tube that wouldn't stick to anything. He'd been looking for something else—but the stuff became Teflon.

- **C.F. Schonbein** discovered an important explosive through the same process. He was working with nitric acid in his wife's kitchen—a no-no—while she was away on a shopping trip. And spilled some. He quickly grabbed his wife's cotton apron (which just happened to be nearby), and wiped up the mess. Then he hung the apron over the stove to dry. But instead of drying properly, it disintegrated. By accident, Schonbein had discovered nitrocellulose, which eventually became a substitute for gunpowder.

- **Two U.S. Navy technicians** were trying to test a radio communications channel across the Potomac River when a passing steamer got in the way. The ship bounced the radio signal right back at the men. As they considered what had happened, they developed the idea of radar.

The Knowledge to See

It's not enough just to live off the benefits of serendipity, though. The process of serendipity must happen a hundred times for every time it leads to new creative thought. Why? The reason is simple enough: **it works only when you have the background to know what you're looking at.**

Louis Pasteur described what I'm talking about: **"Success favors the prepared mind."**

When life hands you a lemon, make lemonade!

Mental Practice

Before becoming president of the United States, Abraham Lincoln imagined what he would say and do as president.

One good way to solve a creative problem is to mentally practice coming to the solution to that problem.

This process of mental practice has long been recognized as a helpful one. Through mental practice we can approach a difficult challenge and conquer it. Then we can take what we experienced and learned mentally and apply it physically.

Picture This

The more we picture things in our minds, the more our minds will accept the picture as reality.

- One woman proved to herself how well mental practice works when she took a trip to England. She was concerned about driving on the left side of the road, and decided to mentally rehearse the procedure. On the flight across the Atlantic, she pictured herself sitting in a car with the steering wheel on the right side. She drove along the side of the road, passing other cars, executing difficult turns, moving onto one-way streets, moving back out into traffic. When she finally arrived, the car was just like an old friend. She'd driven it many times before, in her mind.

- Dr. Charles Mayo recognized the importance of mental rehearsal in his medical practice. Whenever he was faced with a troublesome surgery, he'd seek a few minutes' solitude so he could go over the procedure in his mind. He'd picture to himself the process of cutting into the flesh; he'd hear himself asking for the instruments, in sequence; he'd feel each instrument snug in his hand as he applied it to the operation.

- One of America's most famous attorneys, Clarence Darrow, did the same thing. He'd rehearse important cases mentally before he ever stood before judge and jury. He'd speak his arguments, show his evidence, counteract his opponent's expected strategies. He became so effective that his name is remembered even today, nearly fifty years after his death.

Several years ago mental practice became so well known that some scientists decided to test it out. Somehow it didn't seem reasonable that mental practice could make that big of a difference.

The results of their experiment were reported in *Research Quarterly.* They recruited a bunch of students and divided them up into three groups. The first group was to practice throwing basketball free throws every day for twenty days.

The second group wasn't to practice at all. The third group was to practice mentally only.

Each group was scored on the first and last days, to measure their improvement. And the results were astounding.

The first group, which practiced every day, improved by 24 percent.

The second group, which didn't practice at all, didn't improve at all.

The third group, which practiced mentally only, improved by 23 percent.

The researchers concluded that practicing mentally is virtually as effective as actual physical practice.

Alex Morrison is a famous golf instructor who authored the book, *Better Golf Without Practice*. His method is mental rehearsal, rather than actual practice out on the links. He teaches his students the basic strokes, then instructs them to spend at least five minutes a day playing perfect golf in their imaginations.

Through that process they're able to improve their scores by 10 to 12 strokes—without ever hitting the ball!

Says Morrison of the method: "You must have a clear mental picture of the correct thing before you can do it successfully."

Mental picturing works as well in creativity as in any other field. When we consider *any* problem in our minds, visualizing it repeatedly, we can solve that problem in the real world much more easily.

Dr. John C. Eccles and Sir Charles Sherrington, experts in brain physiology, explain: **"When you learn anything, a pattern of neurons forming a chain is set up in your brain tissue. This chain, or electrical pattern, is your brain's method of remembering. So since the subconscious cannot distinguish a real from an imagined experience, perfect mental practice can change, or correct, imperfect electrical patterns grooved there."**

"First learn how to do whatever you want to do properly through instruction . . . then mentally visualize yourself doing it properly . . . five minutes at a time . . . whenever the time presents itself. Mental practice works."

Earl Nightingale

One good way to obtain a relaxed state: tense, then relax, each part of your body in its turn.

A Tool for Opening Your Creative Mind

Object analogy is a process of making ordinary objects give us answers to our problems. We take a look at a leaf, a shoe, a rock, a book, and suddenly we make an analogy to our problem. We see how a book is like the problem we're trying to solve—and the book helps us to find the answer.

Sometimes the insights for solving problems lie right under our noses. The pencil is an example of how object analogy works to produce creative thinking.

Problem: How can I improve my marriage?

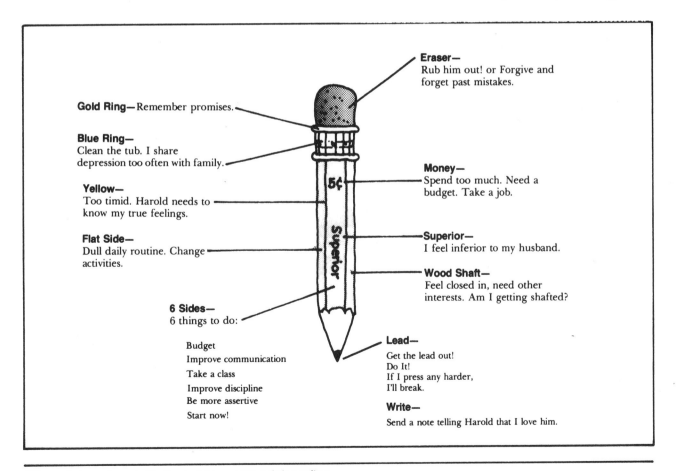

Eraser—
Rub him out! or Forgive and forget past mistakes.

Gold Ring—Remember promises.

Blue Ring—
Clean the tub. I share depression too often with family.

Money—
Spend too much. Need a budget. Take a job.

Yellow—
Too timid. Harold needs to know my true feelings.

Superior—
I feel inferior to my husband.

Flat Side—
Dull daily routine. Change activities.

Wood Shaft—
Feel closed in, need other interests. Am I getting shafted?

6 Sides—
6 things to do:

Budget
Improve communication
Take a class
Improve discipline
Be more assertive
Start now!

Lead—
Get the lead out!
Do It!
If I press any harder, I'll break.

Write—
Send a note telling Harold that I love him.

Object analogies can be used with all sorts of things: a tree, a chair, a radio, a car, a toaster, a hand—you name it!

When Galileo saw a simple magnifying toy, something clicked in his brain. His mind made an analogy, and he saw how he could make a tool to study the universe.

Einstein was trying to think through some difficult aspects of the theory of relativity when he happened to see a record player. Ah-ha! He saw the analogy, the relationship of the moving record to the stationary needle—and was able to understand things as he never had before.

The small and insignificant things in life that surround us often give insight into solving big and important problems.

Little Things Can Mean A Lot

The small and insignificant things in life sometimes give us insight into big and important problems. Who would have thought that a pencil could serve as an object analogy for improving a marriage? Yet, once a close look is taken, the object is incredibly instructive.

"An inventor's power to invent depends on his ability to see analogies between results."

David Page

Sometimes creativity may just be a matter of getting rid of something.

How to Get More From Your Dreams

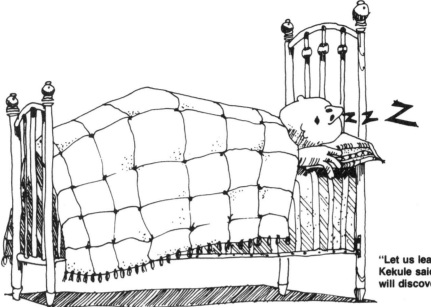

"Let us learn how to dream," Kekule said, "and perhaps we will discover the truth."

Some of our best ideas come from dreams. Most of us spend about one-third of our lives in bed—or 210,240 hours in a normal life span. A measurable portion of that time is spent dreaming. What if we could tap into that tremendous store of time and come out with creative answers? We'd have a storehouse of ideas that could make the difference between creativity and mediocrity.

When we consciously use our dreams for ideas, we end up being more creative.

- Author **J.B. Priestly** came up with ideas for three important essays through dreams: "The Berkshire Beast," "The Strange Outfitter," and "The Dream."

- **Ray Bradbury,** one of the most popular science fiction writers of all time, is a proponent of creativity through dreams: "Quite often I do discover some preciously good material in the half-awakened, half-slumbery time before real sleep. Quite often I have forced myself completely awake to make notes on ideas thus come upon."

- German scientist **Friedrich Kekule** spent years, unsuccessfully, trying to discover the structure of the benzene molecule. Then one night he had a dream about a snake writhing in a circle. When he awoke he thought of the dream, and realized the circle was really a hexagon. In a flash of insight, he realized that the molecular structure he'd been seeking was a hexagon. His pronouncement is considered one of the most brilliant pieces of prediction in the history of organic chemistry.

To get great ideas, use this wonderful device: it's called a pillow!

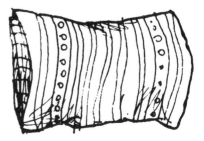

- It was through a dream that **Neils Bohr,** a noted physicist, was able to conceive his model of the atom.

- **Robert Louis Stevenson** discovered that he could dream complete stories—and then change them in subsequent dreams if he wasn't satisfied with them.

- **Elias Howe** spent many years trying to perfect his sewing machine. But he was stumped about how to attach the thread to the needle. Then he had a dream. In the dream he was given twenty-four hours to complete his invention. If he failed, he'd be killed by cannibals with their deadly spears.

He worked feverishly to meet the deadline, but still couldn't overcome that one obstacle of the needle. The cannibals surrounded him and slowly raised their spears. As they descended, Howe noticed that all the spears had small holes in their tips.

He awoke sweating—but still alive. And now he knew what to do. He'd put a hole in the end of the needle!

A Friend's Experience

A friend was once struggling with a problem as a designer. He tried and tried to resolve his design problem, but the solution wouldn't come.

Then one night he went to sleep and had a dream. He dreamed he was trying to catch a fish—but he was attempting to put the bait on a straight hook. When the bait hit the water, it slipped right off and sank to the bottom. This happened over and over again, and he never was able to catch the fish.

When he awoke he realized that the dream gave him the answer to his problem. All he had to do, he said, was to make one small change in his design—as small as bending a straight hook—and suddenly everything worked.

The Metaphorical Message

Dreams are usually metaphorical, and they should be interpreted that way. Fishing had nothing to do with the design problem, but it did symbolize the problem. If we interpret the actual representations of a dream, we may totally misunderstand. But if we interpret the symbols (which is how the subconscious mind apparently communicates with the conscious mind in dreams), we may find some creative answers to our problems.

"Second time tonight I've had this silly dream!"

"Stephen Foster dreamed of Jeannie with the light brown hair, Byron of things that are, and Poe of dreams that no mortal ever dreamed before."

Earl Nightingale

How to Use Dreams Creatively

The power of dreams isn't limited to inventors or writer or scientists. We can all use dreams creatively to solve the problems we face. Here are some steps that have been proven to work:

1. Before you go to sleep, put a pad and pencil near your bed. Tell yourself to think about the problem or situation you're concerned about—and to awaken after you've finished the dream.(With practice, your subconscious mind will obey your conscious desires.)

2. Go to sleep. ZZZZZZZZZZZ.

3. When the dream is finished, wake up—but don't open your eyes. Visual input will disturb your mind. Review the dream.

4. Open your eyes and write down the main elements of the dream. Dreams fade quickly. Too many people say, 'Boy, that was so important I'll surely remember it in the morning'—and then forget it totally. Don't make that mistake. Write it down.

Special Note

The conscious mind often erects barriers against symbols and metaphors, but the subconscious doesn't suffer from that. In fact, the subconscious mind seems to be more comfortable with metaphors than the more concrete things of life.

Since that's the case, we can help the subconscious mind out as it gets ready to dream. Before you go to sleep, think about your problem, then ask the subconscious mind to bring you an animal in your sleep to give you the answer.

The subconscious mind likes metaphor—so you can prime it with a metaphor (the animal) of your own.

"Some of my best ideas come to me in my dreams."
Norman Alexander, Sculptor

5. Go back to sleep. Don't worry about what you've dreamed. The paper will remember it for you.

6. In the morning, go over your notes and fill in the gaps. Write down such details as setting, colors, textures, smells, attitudes, and precise visual images.

Fruit From Nuts

Here's what business managers are saying about their creative people:

"Every once in a while, the boys in the back will come up with a halfway decent idea. Other than that they should probably all be canned."

"Perkes looks like he never does anything. He just sits there all day. Oh, he came out with that brilliant circuit design, but that was a fluke."

"They're so demanding! And when they're not asleep they're totally spaced out."

"We spend entirely too much on R&D."

"Stenski comes up with a few good ideas, but don't give them too much credence—she's a woman."

"Sure, they solved our problem. But it was so simple anyone could have come up with *that* answer."

The problem with most leaders is that they love the fruit but hate the tree. They like to be able to innovate. Many know that to fail to innovate is to die. But they have a hard time with their creative people. Innovators are often unmanageable. They're unpredictable. They're disorderly and disrespectful. You can't plan around them.

You try to order them around and their productivity drops.

Try to get rid of the tree, though, and suddenly you don't have its fruit anymore. **You've got to have both.**

Innovators may seem to be a little fruity sometimes—but that fruitiness is worth the results gained.

Inside that nut may be a highly creative—and valuable—person.

Hard Work?

What's wrong with this picture?

Ah! the joys of creativity...lounging under an apple tree, shady and comfortable. An apple drops down and bonks the creator on the head. Voila! An inspiration!

Or maybe you're sitting at your desk, feet up. All of a sudden, out of the blue, with no prior preparation, a brilliant idea comes into your head. It will make you a million!

The view of creativity as an easy, contemplative effort is commonly held by a heck of a lot of people. And every one of them is wrong!

Creativity Is Hard Work

It takes a lot of effort over many hours and years to produce something that's truly worthwhile. A person who hopes to be creative must consign himself to the hard facts of life: **It takes creative effort to produce creative results.** With an emphasis on the word *effort*.

Michelangelo said, "If people knew how hard I worked to get my mastery, it wouldn't seem so wonderful after all."

Einstein was asked for a listing of his forebears, in an effort to discover the origins of his genius. He replied, "As far as my forebears, my ancestors, first of all I know virtually nothing about them—nobody alive can say much about them—and if there were talents or gifts among them they could not, because of the restricted conditions of life, express themselves. Moreover, I know quite certainly that I myself have no special gift. Curiosity, obsession, and dogged endurance combined with self-critique have brought me my ideas."

Said Edison, "Genius is one percent inspiration and ninety-nine percent perspiration."

And Alexander Hamilton: "Men give me credit for some genius. All the genius I have lies in this; when I have a subject in hand, I study it profoundly. Day and night it is before me. My mind becomes pervaded with it. Then the effort which I have made is what people are pleased to call the fruit of genius. It is the fruit of labor and thought."

"Genius is the capacity for taking infinite pains."
Thomas Carlyle

"How do I work? I grope."
Albert Einstein

"A genius? Perhaps, but before I was a genius I was a drudge."
Ignace Paderewski

51

Two Brains in One Skull

The brain is made up of two parts, and each part has different functions. The left side of the brain is logical and linear, and that's the side we start with when we begin to solve a problem. But the left side can take us only so far, and then our thinking shifts to the right side of the brain. The right side is more creative and nonlinear. It takes the data the left brain processed and looks at it creatively.

Only by utilizing both sides of our brains can we solve problems creatively. The brain will automatically shift back and forth from left to right if we'll let it. But if we try to force it to stay logical and linear, we'll fail to receive the benefits of the brain's creative capacities.

Here's a model of how split-brain problem solving works:

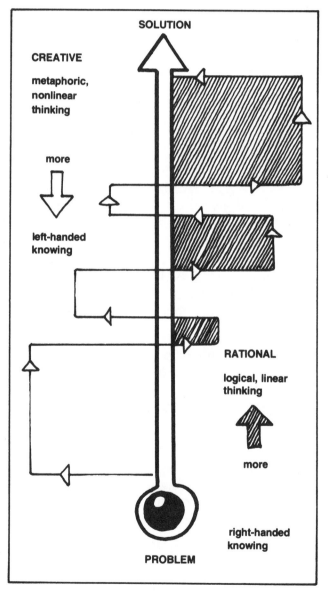

Using BOTH sides of the brain is the key to true creativity.

This model was created by Bob Samples, *The Metaphoric Mind,* Addison-Wesley, 1976.

Why It Is So Hard To Get Your Ideas Accepted

You work your brains out and your fingers off and now you have a great new idea that's going to make a million. But wait; don't forget to be realistic. There are always barriers to selling your ideas to other people.

There are the two main reasons. First, many firms are distrustful of anything they haven't been involved with from the beginning. Second, people absolutely hate hassle. Let's talk about both:

People often invest their ego in doing things the same old way. In addition, the leader has many support people whose entire jobs are devoted to preserving the status quo.

1. **NIH (Not Invented Here) Syndrome.** The NIH mentality applies almost everywhere. A company has its own shop. They have their own R&D set-up. Anyone coming in from the outside just *can't* know what he's talking about.

I was once part of a group that made a presentation to an auto company. The company was having problems and needed help—enough to ask for it. But when we gave them our ideas, we met a solid wall of resistance. They resented the idea that we would think we could solve problems they couldn't. In the end, they rejected just about everything we had to say—all because of NIH!

When Bell Labs invented the transistor, anyone with his eyes open would have seen it was the wave of the future. But American companies would hardly even consider using transistors. They had too much of an investment in tubes—and, besides, "Transistors can't be any good; they were Not Invented Here!"

The Japanese didn't suffer from NIH. They snatched at the opportunity to have a great new technology and got the jump on everyone else.

2. **Hassle.** That one word says volumes. Everyone and his mother-in-law wants to avoid

A good time to overcome natural resistance is when the people involved are making a key change anyway—a new company, new department, new direction.

hassle, and companies are no exception. New ideas all too often just invite trouble. Start looking at someone's idea and you're inviting a lawsuit. He may claim you stole his idea—even if you have been developing the same thing for the last seven years.

More than one big movie producer is presently being sued by some small guy out in Boise or Rapid City or Tallahassee. The small guy claims the producer stole his idea.

Ideas are never totally unique. Often it's simply easier for a company to refuse to look at any new idea than to face the possibility of *hassle*.

Outside ideas invariably have to overcome difficult barriers before they'll even be considered.

How do you overcome those barriers? I know an inventor who's had a pretty good batting average at selling his ideas. He's learned that success in selling ideas narrows down to two things:

**who you know;
who knows you.**

If you can meet the right people and develop their confidence, you'll have a much greater chance at overcoming the obstacles to outside ideas.

This is the best approach to getting your idea accepted within any organization.

A Logical Creative Technique

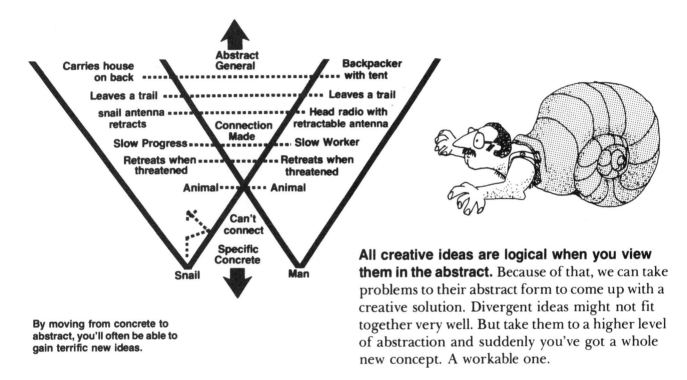

By moving from concrete to abstract, you'll often be able to gain terrific new ideas.

Labels in diagram:
- Abstract General
- Specific Concrete
- Carries house on back
- Leaves a trail
- snail antenna retracts
- Slow Progress
- Retreats when threatened
- Animal
- Snail
- Connection Made
- Can't connect
- Backpacker with tent
- Leaves a trail
- Head radio with retractable antenna
- Slow Worker
- Retreats when threatened
- Animal
- Man

Most often our minds work logically. Emotions are part of everything we do, but it's logic that we base most of our creative decisions on. Our logical decisions might not make sense to anyone else, but to us they're completely sensible.

For example, if someone said that marbles are like oil, you might think he has a few marbles in his head. Yet when you understand what he means, you see that his statement is totally logical.

Envision lubricating oil as millions of tiny marbles sandwiched between two surfaces. Suddenly it all makes sense.

All creative ideas are logical when you view them in the abstract. Because of that, we can take problems to their abstract form to come up with a creative solution. Divergent ideas might not fit together very well. But take them to a higher level of abstraction and suddenly you've got a whole new concept. A workable one.

An Example

You'll note that I've given an example above of how it works. The *V*s outline two divergent lines of thought—and how they correlate in the abstract. At the bottom of the *V*s, the man and the snail have nothing in common. But look what happens as they're considered in more and more abstract terms.

"The capacity to see the essence of a generality depends on the skill of abstraction."

W.J.J. Gordon

Toll Position—
Keep the Money Coming

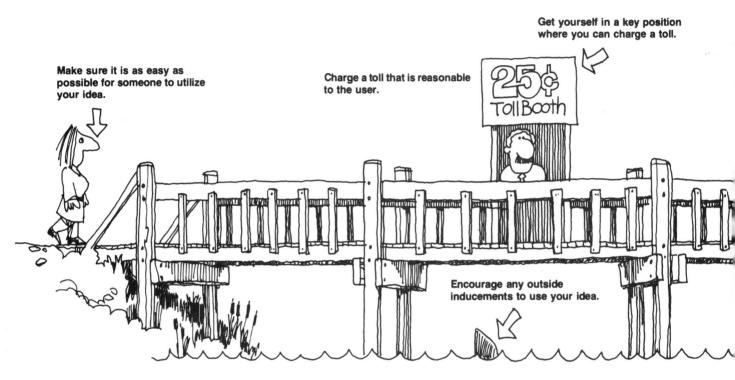

Make sure it is as easy as possible for someone to utilize your idea.

Charge a toll that is reasonable to the user.

Get yourself in a key position where you can charge a toll.

25¢ Toll Booth

Encourage any outside inducements to use your idea.

You're driving down a new road. Nice and easy. Then you see a row of booths across the road. Oh-oh. You have to stop and pay a toll to use the road. You dig deep and pull out your quarter. You're not sure you want to pay, but that's the only way they'll let you drive on the road. So probably it's worth it.

The city planners put up a bridge. They don't want to charge all the taxpayers—just those who use the bridge. How do they do it? They charge a toll. You dig deep for another quarter.

Tolls are great inventions. They're so great that everyone should try to get a toll bridge or road all his own.

That's what innovators should do. Get in a toll position. Then every time people use the creation the creator gets paid.

How can you charge a toll? Some examples:

- **royalties** if you're an author, you get paid a percentage on every book of yours that's sold. If you're a songwriter, you get a percentage on every copy of your song that sells. If you own mineral rich land, you get a percentage of every ton of coal they pull out of your land.

- **usage fees** lend some money and you get to charge a percentage every month. Let someone

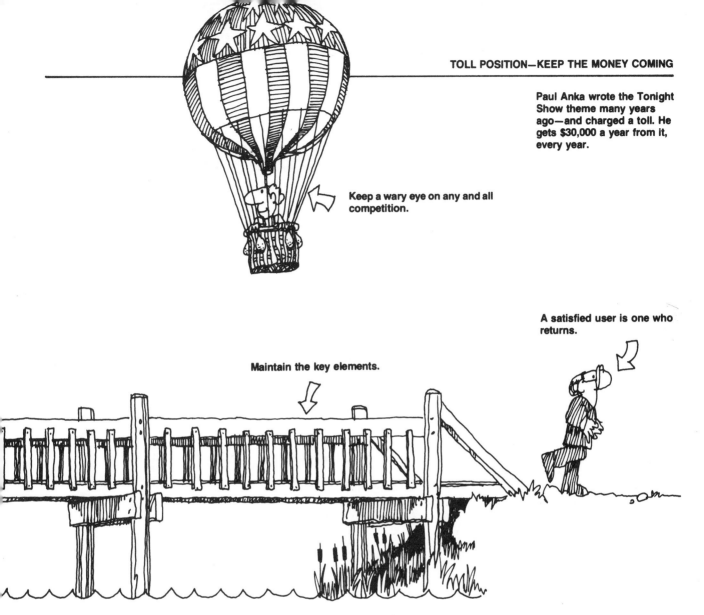

Paul Anka wrote the Tonight Show theme many years ago—and charged a toll. He gets $30,000 a year from it, every year.

Keep a wary eye on any and all competition.

A satisfied user is one who returns.

Maintain the key elements.

rent your apartment and you get a payment every month.

- **appreciation** as time passes, your land or gold grows more valuable; you can charge more for it.

Collecting Payment for Your Idea

Rather than sell your idea outright, get in a toll position. Then you can get regular payments for it, just as if you were collecting a quarter for every car that drives on a toll road. Here's how:

1. Set it up so it will work without effort. Have the people pay for *usage*. Have a royalty contract, usage fee, rental agreement, license requirement, subscription arrangement.

2. Charge your toll for products, services, or a combination of both.

3. Maintain a power position, so you'll be able to control the toll.

4. Remember that tolls are always only temporary—a new road is built, people start to take an alternate route, someone puts up a free bridge next to your toll bridge. Your toll can't last forever, but until it ends, use it for all it's worth.

If you charge a toll every time someone uses your idea, you'll make a lot more money.

Mind Joggers to Increase Creativity

Use checklists to jog your mind into new directions of thought.

"Whenever I go the store, I've got to have a shopping list with me. When I forget, I have a hard time remembering what I'm after. I get sidetracked and buy things I don't really need, and I end up not buying things I do need. Forgetting my list is a real pain in the kazoo!"

Sound familiar? Probably—lists are helpful for all of us. When we have them and use them, we're happy. But when we don't, nothing works.

Idea checklists are the same as shopping lists. The shopping list tells us what aisles to go down and which products to pick up. The idea list helps the mind remember which things to consider, and which ideas are most valuable. When you go shopping for ideas, be sure to take a list with you.

"One single question can jog your mind into that unique creative solution that you desire."

In this section I've included several kinds of lists. Each one has a different use; each will help you in a different way. But overall they have the same purpose: to act as mind-joggers, to jar your brain into thinking of concepts, strategies, conflicts, and ideas that you might otherwise not consider.

When you have a problem you'd like to find a creative solution for, take a look at these lists and find the one that will work best for your situation. Then thoughtfully go over each item on the chosen list.

Problem Sources List

☐ Friends?	☐ Leisure Time?
☐ Family?	☐ Needs?
☐ Neighbors?	☐ Stress Points?
☐ Church?	☐ Pains?
☐ House?	☐ Intersections?
☐ Fears?	☐ Complexities?
☐ School?	☐ Surprises?
☐ Homework?	☐ Mistakes?
☐ Graduation?	☐ Monotony?
☐ Bottlenecks?	☐ Money?
☐ Anxieties?	☐ Plans?
☐ Performance?	☐ Hopes and Desires?
☐ Career?	☐ Routine?
☐ Happiness?	☐ Habits?
☐ Safety?	☐ Pet Peeves?
☐ Waste?	☐ Appearance?
☐ Attitudes?	☐ Improvements?
☐ Goals?	☐ Comfort?
☐ Values?	☐ Complications?
☐ Social Life?	☐ Inefficiencies?
☐ Transportation?	☐ Misunderstandings?
☐ Personality?	☐ Other?

Situations List

- [ ] Who?
- [ ] What?
- [ ] Why Not?
- [ ] When?
- [ ] Where?
- [ ] Why?
- [ ] How?
- [ ] Which?

Objects List

- [ ] Function
- [ ] Structure
- [ ] Substance
- [ ] Taste
- [ ] Size
- [ ] Texture
- [ ] Odor
- [ ] Sound
- [ ] Shape
- [ ] Temperature
- [ ] Time
- [ ] Space
- [ ] Color
- [ ] Magnitude
- [ ] Movement

Acceptance Finding List

- [ ] **Acceptance:** In what way might I gain acceptance?

- [ ] **Anticipation:** How might I overcome anticipated objections?

- [ ] **Assistance:** In what ways might other persons or groups help me?

- [ ] **Locations:** What places or locations might be advantageous?

- [ ] **Timing:** In what ways might I use special times, dates, etc.?

- [ ] **Precautions:** What measures might test my "best" idea? Would your idea still seem sound to you if you were someone else?

Problem Needs List

- [ ] Why?
- [ ] What is the problem?
- [ ] What is the real problem?
- [ ] What are the needs of all the major parts?
- [ ] What is the main need that if not properly satisfied makes fulfilling all the other needs pointless?
- [ ] Which of the needs are . . . vital?
- [ ] . . . very important?
- [ ] . . . important?
- [ ] . . . desirable?
- [ ] . . . unimportant?
- [ ] . . . if the problem is solved—so what?

Possible Tools List

- [ ] Hardware?
- [ ] Software?
- [ ] Group?
- [ ] Individual?
- [ ] A computer?
- [ ] Friends?
- [ ] Enemies?
- [ ] A screwdriver?
- [ ] Inanimate?
- [ ] A book?
- [ ] Expert?
- [ ] Pen and Paper?
- [ ] Mathematics?
- [ ] Mythology?
- [ ] Relatives?
- [ ] Strangers?
- [ ] Emotional?
- [ ] Mental?
- [ ] Physical?
- [ ] Organic?
- [ ] Inorganic?
- [ ] Spiritual?
- [ ] Intellectual?
- [ ] Researcher?
- [ ] History?
- [ ] University?
- [ ] Meditation?
- [ ] Prayer?

- [ ] Who knows what you need to know?
- [ ] Is it in the library or in the stars?

Behind every word is the concept it carries. That concept may be the critical element that will give you your solution.

Idea-Finding Questions List

☐ **Adapt?** New ways to use as is? Other uses if modified?

☐ **Modify?** New twist? Change meaning, color, motion, sound, odor, form, shape? Other changes?

☐ **Magnify?** What to add? More time? Greater frequency? Stronger? Higher? Longer? Thicker? Extra value? Add ingredient? Duplicate? Multiply? Exaggerate?

☐ **Minimize?** Subtract? Make it smaller? Condense? Miniature? Lower? Shorter? Lighter? Omit? Streamline? Split up? Understate?

☐ **Substitute?** Who else instead? What else instead? Other ingredient? Other material? Other process? Other power? Other place? Other approach? Other tone of voice?

☐ **Rearrange?** Interchange components? Other pattern? Other layout? Other sequence? Transpose cause and effect? Change pace? Change schedule? Eliminate?

☐ **Reverse?** Transpose positive and negative? How about opposites? Turn it backward? Turn it upside down? Reverse roles? Change shoes? Turn tables? Turn other cheek?

☐ **Combine?** How about a blend, an alloy, an assortment, an ensemble? Combine units? Combine purposes? Combine appeals? Combine ideas? Standardize?

What are the results of your ideas in 10, 15, or 100 years? Predict the ideal answer. Weigh and compare your solutions with those of a five-year-old.

Solution Finding— Solution Evaluation List

☐ Effect on objective?

☐ Individual and/or groups affected?

☐ Cost involved?

☐ Tangibles involved (materials, equipment, etc.)?

☐ Intangibles involved (opinions, attitudes, feelings, aesthetic values, etc)?

☐ Moral or legal implications?

☐ New problems caused?

☐ Difficulties of implementation and follow up?

☐ Repercussions of failure?

☐ Timeliness?

Others?

☐ What could you put off without it mattering?

☐ What would matter if you put it off?

☐ If you continue going in the direction you're headed, where will it take you?

☐ Are you making a decision too quickly? too slowly?

☐ Compare with other similar situations.

☐ Think from the end to the beginning.

☐ Think in other dimensions.

☐ Are you just repeating yourself?

☐ Are you just repeating yourself?

A word can trigger your mind into action.

6

Some other sources that may help trigger an idea: scriptures, dictionary, thesaurus, almanac, encyclopedia, telephone book, and book indexes.

How Mother Nature Can Increase Creativity

Some of the greatest creativity comes from good old Mother Nature. Mother knows what's best—and those people who follow her lead usually end up ahead of the game.

In nature the name of the game is survival of the fittest. Because of this, plants and animals and insects and bacteria and everything else have been forced to adapt, taking the most advantageous forms. Nature invariably takes the forms that *work*.

Whenever you are faced with a difficult problem, look to nature to see how it solved that same kind of problem. The resulting ideas could save you a lot of creative time—and it could give you an answer you wouldn't get otherwise.

Alexander Graham Bell learned from nature: he modeled the telephone after the human ear.

Using Mother

Examples of people who have successfully used this approach are many:

- Sir March Brumel, for example, solved the problem of underwater construction by watching a shipworm tunneling into a timber. The worm constructed a tube for itself as it moved forward. Watching these worms gave Brumel the idea of using caissons (watertight chambers) for underwater construction.

- Alexander Graham Bell, inventor of the telephone, once recalled,"It struck me that the bones of the human ear were very massive, indeed, as compared with the delicate thin membrane that operated them, and the thought occurred that if a membrane so delicate could move bones so relatively massive, why should not a thicker and stouter piece of membrane move my piece of steel." By understanding the functions of the organs of speech and hearing, Bell was able to invent a tool to send sound electrically over a wire.

Sketches of the heart, from
Leonardo da Vinci's notebook.

- **Camouflage,** the act of concealment, has been used by all kinds of creatures for millennia. Then military personnel thought of copying the approach to hide tanks and cannons and trucks and soldiers.

- **The hypodermic needle** is patterned after the fangs of a rattlesnake. The reptile injects its venom through a hole running down the center of its tooth.

- **Submarines** use the principle of the fish's swimbladder for underwater ballast. The fish inflates and deflates its swimbladder with gas to change its depth in the water.

- Artist and inventor Leonardo da Vinci's secret in creating his deluge of inventions and ideas was to observe nature. His notebooks and sketchbooks contain hundreds of detailed drawings of birds, fish, human organs, human figures, plants, and so on. He saw nature in minute detail and then imitated it in his inventions, which were centuries ahead of their time.

Natural Examples, Technological Inventions

The previous examples are just the beginning. Look at these ways in which nature has inspired man:

- **Modern automatic focus** and exposure cameras are patterned after the human eye.

- **Evaporative air conditioners** work just like a desert jackrabbit's ears, which are coolers that dissipate heat and enable the rabbits to survive in the high desert temperatures.

- **Modern radar** uses ultrasonic waves just as bats have done since the beginning. The bat's system is better than man's, though. It can't be jammed, and some bats can locate fish under the water.

- **A frog's eye** sees only certain things, such as insects that would make good meals. Inspired by this idea, military scientists are trying to invent devices that will see only targets and will disregard all distractions.

- **Velcro** was invented after a Swiss engineer made a careful study of the clinging burdock burr, which grabs onto fabric and won't let go.

- **The jet airplane** uses propulsion to travel through the air much as the squid uses it in water.

Writers and poets have long recognized the beauty and appropriateness found in nature. Henry Thoreau, the American essayist and philosopher, spent years studying nature and meditating about life in general. His writings contain great wisdom and hints for us to live by. Aesop, a Greek writer of fables who lived 620-560 B.C., to express his thought wrote of animals having human characteristics. The number of musical compositions directly inspired by nature are too many to count.

Learning from Nature

Many inventions have been created by trying to imitate nature. The dialysis machine, the electronic computer, and aircraft wings are mechanical replicas of a kidney, the human brain, and a bird's wing.

Use the principles found in nature to help you get good ideas. If things have worked well in nature for eons, why wouldn't they work well for you?

A science has been developed to utilize this idea of borrowing from nature. It's called *bionics*—and it's much more than creating artificial hands and legs. The dictionary defines bionics as "a science concerned with the application of data about the functioning of biological systems to the solution of engineering problems."

"Before he can create, man must have a deep awareness of the world about him—he must be able to really see, hear, feel, touch, and move."

Harold A. Rothbart

Ah Ha!

When we enjoy a sudden flash of insight, we experience the "Ah ha!" principle at work.

"Ah ha!" is what you feel at a sudden burst of knowledge. It describes that eureka stage of creative thinking when the answer you've been looking for becomes clear in your mind. Creative ideas or the answers to problems don't always come to mind while you actively concentrate on them. Instead they often appear when least expected. Important discoveries have burst forth from great minds while the people involved were playing games, taking walks or doing other things not related to the specific problem.

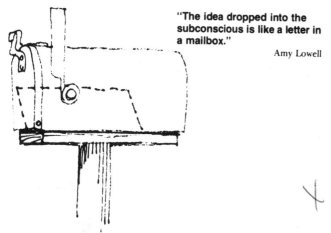

"The idea dropped into the subconscious is like a letter in a mailbox."

Amy Lowell

Flashes of Insight

"Ah ha!" ideas come as flashes of unexpected insight, as bolts out of the blue. Invariably they come after the conscious mind has ceased work on a problem, allowing the subconscious to work on it.

Charles Darwin, originator of the theory of natural selection, wasn't reading a book in his laboratory when his idea for *The Origin of Species* came to him. Instead, he was riding in his carriage. "I can remember the very spot in the road, whilst in my carriage, when to my joy the solution occurred to me," wrote Darwin.

"As I went along, thinking nothing in particular, only looking at things around me and following the progress of the seasons, there would flow into my mind, with sudden and unaccountable emotion, sometimes a line or two of verse, sometimes a whole stanza at once."

A. E. Housman

Bertrand Russell described his approach this way: "I have found, for example, that if I have to write upon some rather difficult topic, the best plan is to think about it with very great intensity—the greatest intensity of which I am capable—for a few hours or days, and at the end of that time give orders, so to speak, (to my subconscious mind) that the work is to proceed underground. After some months I return consciously to the topic and find that the work has been done. Before I had discovered this technique, I used to spend the intervening months worrying because I was making no progress. I arrived at the solution none the sooner for this worry, and the intervening months were wasted, whereas now I can devote them to other pursuits."

Time and again creative people have extolled the workings of the "Ah ha!" principle. It works for problems in writing and arithmetic, for problems in music composition and scientific inquiry. It works for the average person as well as the genius.

"I believe in intution and inspiration; at times I feel certain I am right while not knowing the reason."

Albert Einstein

Using the "Ah ha!" method is like laying and hatching a big egg. Here's how to make it work:

Put "Ah Ha!" to Work for You!

1. Form the egg. Turn the problem over and over in your mind. Look at it from every angle. Consider all possible solutions or ideas. Study it—read books, ask knowledgeable people. Form the problem into a complete and understandable whole. Inspiration doesn't come to an individual unless he has immersed himself in the problem.

2. Lay the egg. It takes a lot of effort to lay an egg and considerable patience waiting for it to hatch. Laying an egg involves a chicken completely, and the creation of your idea should involve you completely. For a while the problem should involve you intensely. But the time must come when you leave the idea alone. Drop it from conscious thought and turn it over to the subconscious.

3. Sit on it. Completely forget about it for now. Let your conscious mind rest. The subconscious mind is like an automated machine that can be turned on and left on alone—it works while the conscious mind is busy doing other things.

4. "Ah ha!" Incubating eggs takes different amounts of time for different eggs. A kiwi egg requires 80 days, a chicken egg 21 days, and a platypus egg only 10 days. Your creative solution will hatch when it is ready. If it emerges before it is mature, shove it back into your mind and keep it warm until it's ready. When your idea finally hatches, bells will ring, lights will flash, and bands will play in your mind. (Or conversely, you may simply say, "Of course. Why didn't I think of that before?")

5. Write your creative thought down. When an idea emerges, keep a record of it. After your mental work has hatched an idea, pin it to a piece of paper. Apply it after you have detailed it in writing.

"Inspiration, then, is the impulse which sets creation in movement; it is also the energy which keeps it going."

Roger Sessions

Getting a good idea is often like laying an egg: first you lay it; then you sit on it for a while.

Creative Solutions Made to Order

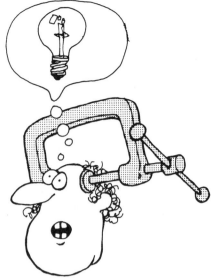

"We do it by changing an attribute or a quality of something, or else by applying that same quality or attribute to some other thing."

Robert P. Crawford

One good way of finding a creative solution to a problem is to force connections. Here's how to force connections:

1. Clearly state your problem.

2. List all the attributes of your problem.

3. Consider attributes for which you have a solution—even if it's in another application.

4. Make links (force connections) between the attributes of your problem and the solutions you noted in step three.

Emergency Alert System

A town in the western U.S. decided to check its emergency alert system. At the appointed time, the switches were thrown on the large sirens throughout the city. Civil Defense personnel took their posts, as instructed, to help the frenzied public that would surely be rushing in to the shelters.

But no one came. The experiment was a total flop.

What was the problem? First, many of the sirens malfunctioned, and didn't issue a single sound. Second, people who *did* hear the warning were confused. They didn't know what to do.

The city officials definitely had a problem on their hands. With forced connections they might have come to a workable solution:

1. State the problem:

   We need a reliable way to warn people of approaching danger.

2. List the attributes of the problem:

- must locate the people

- must get their attention

- must give the message

- must get the desired reaction from the public

3. Write the various ways each attribute of the problem has been solved:

LOCATE PEOPLE	GET ATTENTION	DELIVER MESSAGE	OBTAIN DESIRED REACTION
Homes	Bells	Telephone	Find Safety
Schools	Sirens	Advertise	Seek Help
Cars	Whistles	Outdoor Sirens	Find Protection
Offices	Mass Media	Bells	Inform
In Transit	P.A. Systems	P.A. Systems	All of above
Parks	Bright Colors	Print	
	Bright Lights	Radio—TV	

4. Link the attributes to form new solutions.

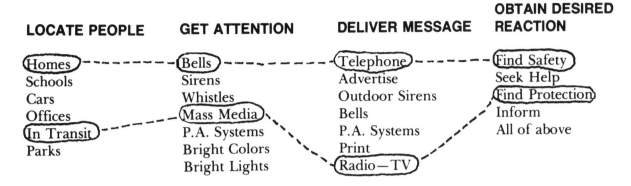

LOCATE PEOPLE	GET ATTENTION	DELIVER MESSAGE	OBTAIN DESIRED REACTION
Homes	Bells	Telephone	Find Safety
Schools	Sirens	Advertise	Seek Help
Cars	Whistles	Outdoor Sirens	Find Protection
Offices	Mass Media	Bells	Inform
In Transit	P.A. Systems	P.A. Systems	All of above
Parks	Bright Colors	Print	
	Bright Lights	Radio—TV	

Once you've forced new connections, you can see a number of ways the city officials could have solved their problem. For example:

Make an arrangement with the telephone company to cause all the telephones throughout the city to ring. When answered, the phones would relay a pre-recorded message instructing people what to do.

Employ a mass-media advertising campaign that tells of the danger alert system and how it works.

Fix the sirens so that the people would hear them. This must be coordinated with some sort of mass communication to explain how the danger alert system works and what people should do when alerted.

Work out a special mass-media danger alert system that would automatically interrupt scheduled radio and TV programming with a pre-recorded message of approaching danger.

There are many other kinds of solutions that are possible. See if you can expand the list of attributes, find new connections among attributes, and find new solutions.

Problem? Design a new kind of chair

MATERIAL	BONDING	SHAPE	CUSHION	LOCATION
Wood	Screws & Glue	Perpendicular Plans	Fabric	Kitchen
Cement	Magnets	Round Balls	Metal	Outdoors
Metal Pipes	Gravity	Flat	Marshmallows	Bath
Bone	Hope	Cubes	Stone	Freeway
Water	Springs	Organic	Jello	Underwater
			Play-dough	

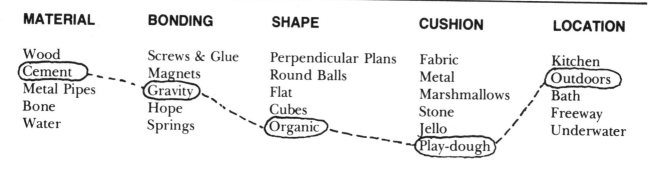

MATERIAL	BONDING	SHAPE	CUSHION	LOCATION
Wood	Screws & Glue	Perpendicular Plans	Fabric	Kitchen
Cement	Magnets	Round Balls	Metal	Outdoors
Metal Pipes	Gravity	Flat	Marshmallows	Bath
Bone	Hope	Cubes	Stone	Freeway
Water	Springs	Organic	Jello	Underwater
			Play-dough	

Result:

A chair formed by sitting on a bag of wet cement. Like play dough, when it's dry it will be specially molded to fit your rump.

Whenever you're struggling with a difficult problem, see if you can find a creative solution by using the approach of forced connections. The things you're comparing may seem unrelated, but by forcing links between them, you can often come up with some surprising—and very workable—ideas.

This matrix will help you to force connections as you work on some of your own creative problems.

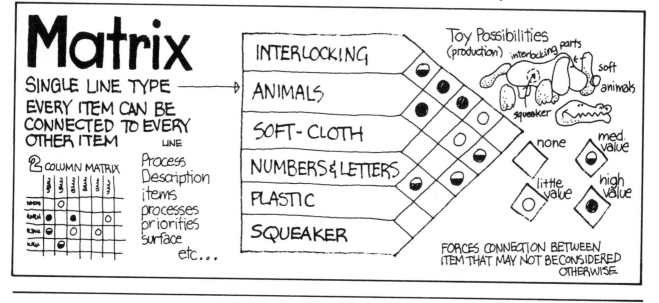

A
Creative Thinking Technique That Never Fails

How is the problem like a violin or a sunflower?

Metaphors are a good way of developing creativity. They bring order to our ideas. They give us something understandable to hook on to what we don't understand.

A metaphor compares the meaning and attributes of one thing to the meaning and attributes of something else.

We use metaphors all the time, often without even thinking about it:

- Grandma is a real brick.

- Getting him to change is like moving a boulder.

- You can't offend him; he's really thick-skinned.

- I can read her like a book.

- She comes and goes like the wind.

- The larger the island of knowledge, the longer the shore of wonder.

Sometimes your metaphor will seem absurd. But it's the absurdity that will get the mind going, that will start the creative juices flowing. State the metaphor—then try to justify it.

Maintaining a friendship is like living on a small planet. That's the metaphor. How can it be true? We survive on the planet balanced between gravity holding us down and centrifugal force throwing us out. Friendship works the same way. we maintain a delicate balance between being pulled too close and being thrown apart. By making the metaphor, we're able to understand both friendship and planets better.

Nature has been the prime source of our technological revolution. The future may mean nature will be copied even more.

"The active process leading to creativity appears to be metaphoric in nature."

Don Fabun

69

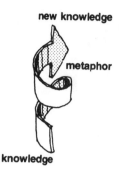

A learning spiral—using the known to comprehend the unknown, making the unknown part of the known.

new knowledge

metaphor

knowledge

How Metaphor Works

Learning by metaphor works in a spiral. We start with a base of knowledge. Then we move up through the metaphor, comparing what we know to what we don't know. The result is new knowledge, which gives us a new base to work from.

Lord Rutherford was able to expand our understanding of the atom through creative use of the metaphor spiral. He compared the workings of the solar system to the structure of the atom, going from the known to the unknown. His ideas have been refined since his day. But Rutherford's metaphor opened many doors.

Metaphor Brings Growth

The use of suitable metaphors often contributes to significant advances in human knowledge. Without the metaphor, no progress is made. With the metaphor, the researcher or philosopher is able to make a new connection, one that makes the difference to our understanding.

For eons man didn't really know how the heart worked. Alchemists and scientists tried different kinds of explanations, but none was really adequate. Then one day William Harvey was struck with the workings of the fire pump. With that simple metaphor, he was able to expand our understanding—and only then did research into the human circulatory system really become meaningful.

A Creative Tool

We can use the metaphor to help us reach creative solutions, no matter what problem we're working on. The approach is simple: start with what you know. Compare what you know to the problem you're concerned with. Then consider what you learn from the relationship.

"The greatest thing by far is to be a master of metaphor."
Aristotle

Metaphor can be one of the most valuable of all creative tools.

Metaphor

▷ LINKS OLD KNOWLEDGE TO NEW

OLD — a metaphor — NEW

▷ A VEHICLE TO CARRY CONCEPTS

CONCEPTS

The best method to do it

▷ NOT LOGICAL (Breaks the Rules)

▷ TELLS ABOUT OUR KNOWLEDGE OF WHATS REAL

▷ THIS (known) IS LIKE THAT (unknown)

▷ GENERATES NEW IDEAS (causes new ways of seeing)

▷ HAS MULTIPLE MEANINGS (Broad Interpretation)

▷ ALL OUR THINKING IS METAPHORICAL

▷ MATH·LANGUAGE·ART IS A METAPHOR (our whole concept & belief system is metaphorical in nature)

▷ ALL METAPHORS ARE SENSORY

▷ GIVE SIGHT TO THE CONFLICT IN VALUES

▷ A SHARED METAPHOR = A SHARED VISION

▷ GOOD METAPHORS Active Identifiable Simple concise appropriate

▷ GOES THROUGH THE BACK DOOR goes past barriers GETS INSIDE

Beware of the Crackpot in the Basement

Harry Weeks was a crackpot who tinkered in his basement. That's what everyone thought, anyway. He was quiet and secretive—when friends would stop by, he'd never have much to say about his current project. That was just as well; acquaintances weren't really interested anyway.

One night Harry had a dream about a matter transporter. It was a simple enough gadget, but there was nothing simple at all about what it could do. You'd put something in one end and it would come out the other, instantaneously—even if the other end was in another state or country.

Harry laughed it off when he woke up. "It was only a crazy dream," he muttered to himself.

But he couldn't get rid of the idea. Off and on he'd mess with it, making drawings or fiddling with little models.

Until one day, after many years, he suddenly realized he'd made a model that worked! His transporter was made up of two big rings, like hula-hoops. He stood one ring in his living room and stood the other upstairs in his bedroom. Then he took one of his books and stuck it through the ring. The book and his hand disappeared. He dropped the book and pulled out his hand. Something fell on the floor—above his head.

Harry raced up the stairs and looked on the floor. There, right beside the second ring, was the book.

Eureka! It would change the world! His mind raced, thinking of all the things people would be able to accomplish with the help of his ring transporter.

That's when he was introduced to reality. No one would listen to him. No one cared. Harry Weeks was just a crackpot how puttered around in his basement.

Then his big break came. His sister Wilma was newly widowed, and she came by to visit for a couple of weeks. He brought out his ring transporter. She tried to be polite, listening to his explanation of how it worked and nodding as though she understood. But she knew old Harry. He had never been the same since he'd retired. And if he wanted to think he had some magic rings—well, it didn't really hurt anything, did it?

Then Harry stepped through the ring—and disappeared. A moment later he walked down the stairs, a big grin on his face. Wilma rubbed her eyes and started to believe.

It was during Wilma's visit that neighbor Jess Stone stopped by—with his dog. Harry decided to give Jess a first-class demonstration. "Watch this!" he shouted. He grabbed the dog and stuck him through the ring. The dog disappeared instantly.

"Hey, that's quite a trick," Jess exclaimed, laughing. "How'd you do that?"

"Come upstairs with me, and I'll explain," Harry said.

They went upstairs. No dog. Harry raced back downstairs. No dog.

It was only a minor setback. But it was quite some time before Jess forgave him for it.

Wilma had some insurance money, from the death of her dearly beloved (bless his soul). She and Harry made a plan. It was really quite simple, and they both thought it would be kind of fun. They would use the money to generate some interest in Harry's device. Then they could both grow rich and famous.

Wilma bought an airplane ticket to Paris, and flew out with one of the rings in her luggage. Then Harry invited a newspaper man over to his house. He promised him the scoop of the year. At a prearranged time, Harry got the newspaper man to step through his transporter ring. When the man's foot hit ground, he was standing under the Eiffel Tower, where Wilma stood with her ring.

Wilma smiled sweetly at him. "Quite the scoop, isn't it," she said. She folded up her ring, put it in her bag, and left the man standing there with his mouth open.

It didn't take much from that point for Harry to get the financial backing he needed. Soon his transporter rings were in mass production. And before long they had covered the world.

Everything that happened after that is a matter of record. The results of Harry's great technological leap were overwhelmingly positive. The transportation industry was revolutionized. People were able to travel wherever they wished, simply by stepping through their rings.

Oh, there were a few minor problems. General Motors and Ford and Volkswagen and Toyota and Datsun all closed down within the second quarter. Iraq used their rings to invade Israel. One enterprising group took rain from Brazil and transported it to the Sahara Desert, totally upsetting the ecology of the planet.

But, all in all, the transporter was a great success. It did fantastic things for sewage treatment. Harry had an expensive new hotel named after him—people could go there and enjoy all the resorts in the world just from that one hotel. All they had to do was walk out the right door.

Oh, in all fairness it should be mentioned that unemployment in the U.S. rose to 30 percent, because of all the jobs that were eliminated. And immigration became an incredible problem. Not to mention the smuggling trade.

Still, Harry knew that he'd been a great benefactor of the human race. Now he's back in his basement (in his new mansion) tinkering around again. This time he's working on a device that will reverse the ageing process. That will bring mankind a lot of positive benefits too.

Beware of the Crackpot

This fable has a moral. Too often we brush aside the thoughts and abilities of the crackpot in the basement, or his brother in the garage. If anything good is going to come to this generation, we say, it will certainly come from the researchers at the universities, or at least from Bell Labs in a logical, sequential manner. Don't think for a minute that anyone is going to get anywhere without a government grant. It just can't be done!

- But wait! What about Einstein? He seemed just a mediocre civil servant until he got rolling. Then he came up with ideas that changed our view of the universe.

- What about Edison? He tinkered around as a handyman. Then calmly went out and changed nearly everything about our way of life.

- What about the Wright brothers? Dropouts from school, bicycle mechanics, of all things! We wouldn't expect much from them!

And they're not alone. The pages of history are filled with stories of unknown men and women who made a big difference. They were outside of the mainstream; some were big losers—and then, suddenly, they pulled a furry rabbit out of their hats.

- John Harrison invented the marine chronometer. He began his career in the loft of an old barn.

- Inventor John Fitch constructed part of America's first steamboat in the vestry of a church in Philadelphia.

- Cyrus McCormick had an idea for a reaper—but he didn't have a good place to work. Finally he set up shop in an old gristmill.

- A model of the first dry dock ever constructed was put together in an attic.

- For years, an impoverished Pablo Picasso painted in the slums of Paris. Yet the paintings he created have become some of the classics of our century.

- John Bunyan wrote most of *Pilgrim's Progress* while incarcerated in prison.

The list could go on and on. But it's the moral that matters, not the examples. You're not a person of means? So what! You're not recognized in your field? Big deal! Join the list you just read, put your creativity to work and change the world. Like Thomas Alva Edison. Or Albert Einstein. Or old Harry Weeks!

What incomprehensible future is now being thought up by an unheard of person?

Metamorphosis

> "There's no use trying," said Alice. "One can't believe impossible things."
> "I dare say you haven't much practice," said the Queen. "When I was your age, I always did it for half-an-hour a day. Why, sometimes I've believed as many as six impossible things before breakfast."
>
> Lewis Carroll

Mental metamorphosis works like magic when it comes to being creative: **Imagine yourself as being the problem you'd like to solve.**

This method of getting new ideas is much underused. Usually we'll remove ourselves from a problem in order to solve it—we'll look at the germ through a microscope. But with mental metamorphosis, we *become* the germ. How does a germ work? Become one of them and you'll know: move as a germ moves, have its needs and appetites, live as it lives, concern yourself with its special problems. All mentally, of course!

Some great scientific discoveries have come from people who were willing to put themselves right into a problem. Michael Faraday, the founder of the electromagnetic theory, pictured himself as an atom under pressure. Through his creative imaginings, he was able to gain insights that led to his theory.

Einstein daydreamed about what would happen if he could fly through space at the speed of light. He even tried to feel the sensations in his muscles, through vivid imagination. Through working with such mental images, Einstein was able to develop important concepts for his theory of relativity.

Dr. Jekyll and Mr. Hyde practiced this method regularly.

Become electricity racing down the wire or a helicopter taking off.

Helpful hints on how to become a helicopter, electricity, or an atom:

1. Relax in a daydreaming state (half awake, half asleep). Soften the lights and get comfortable.

2. Free yourself from inhibitions. Don't feel silly about imagining yourself to be something you're not. If great thinkers such as Einstein were willing to do this, you can too!

3. Take on all the attributes of what you want to become. Acquire its color, taste, speed, texture, shape, and so on. Feel what it feels. See what it sees. Use your imagination.

4. Place what you have become into desired situations. Notice your reactions. If you are a tire, for example, mentally get on the wheel of a car and ride down the road, feeling the rocks, tight turns, and bumps.

5. Record what your mind experiences. Analyze and define what happens.

"The creative process is any thinking process which solves a problem in an original and useful way."

H. Herbert Fox

How to Gain a Creative Point of View

A little kid will drive you nuts with his questions:

- What if cows had wings?

- What if radios were in your brain?

- What if I were the daddy and you were the kid?

- What if cars could go a million miles an hour?

- What if trees grew down instead of up?

I know more than one mom or dad who has put a clamp on the whole thing: "Enough is enough! No more questions."

But I have a better idea: listen. Kids are the most creative people around. And they're teaching us a great approach to creativity with their constant *what if?* questions.

Part of the reason is that kids have a natural curiosity. Part of the reason is that kids don't pretend to know it all, like a lot of adults do. That keeps their creative inquiries fresh and open. Adults, on the other hand, are often stale and closed.

To be truly creative, become a child again—growing older in wisdom and ability, but remaining childlike in outlook. The resulting point of view is amazingly effective.

Watch a small child pick up a new toy. He'll experiment with it, learning about it from every angle. He'll touch it, sit on it, feel every side, smell it, stick it in his mouth. When he's done, he'll know a lot more about the toy than the adult does who gave it to him. He's willing to test, experiment, create, *feel*—whereas mommy or daddy only sits back and watches and judges.

Children Are Free

A child is free to act naturally. But as people grow older they worry more and more about making mistakes. When they do get a good idea, they crush it because they feel that it's not good enough. Or others crush it for them: "It will never work." "Oh, that's been tried before." "That doesn't fit into the criteria of the matrixes of the diffuse parameters we've established to assure no misformulations."

A fear of failure kills a lot of creativity. But when we're childlike we don't have that fear. Instead we'll wonder and explore simply for the joy of it—and we won't let someone else deter us from our path.

Buckminster Fuller is an excellent example of someone who possesses childlike inquisitiveness. He dared to ask questions like, "What if we designed a more efficient building system?" He then carried his question further: "What in nature is the most efficient structure in enclosing the maximum amount of space with the minimum amount of materials?" His answer: the bubble, or sphere. Resulting from his flexible creativity was the geodesic dome.

Jules Verne kept his ability to be childlike throughout his life. He asked the question, "What if man could go to the moon? How would he go?

Jules Verne asked "What if?"
100 years before man walked
on the moon.

we're part of the 98 percent of all adults who are tired and stale.

When we were little kids we liked to fantasize. *"What if?"* was one of our favorite questions. We lived in castles filled with monsters; we were pioneers fighting our way through the wilderness; we put a blanket over a chair and suddenly we were in a cave.

Those who are able to retain that ability to be childlike, or who can regain it, are the people who are able to really exercise creativity as adults.

Seeing the Obvious

A heavy truck once became lodged under an overpass. Police were trying to get it free, to no avail. A crowd gathered. "Cut off the top of the truck," one old man yelled, only half-joking. "You're going to have to dismantle the bridge," another said. "That baby's in there too tight."

Of course neither of these solutions was really workable. But no one could think of anything else.

Then a little boy stepped forward with his idea. "What if they let the air out of the tires?" he wondered.

Suddenly it was obvious. But it required a childlike attitude, one of open-mindedness to see that even though the truck was stuck at the top, the way to get it loose was at the bottom.

What would he find when he arrived?" His ideas were exciting and stimulating to others. A century later, men *did* walk on the moon, just as Verne had envisioned they would.

Second Nature

One study of creativity showed that only about 2 percent of all adults are truly creative. Ten percent of seven-year-olds are creative. And some 90 percent of all five-year-olds are creative.

What does that tell us? That being creative is second-nature to the very young. But as we grow older, we push our creative urges back, or let them get drained out of us. Before we know it,

"What are the conditions of the creative attitude, of seeing and responding, of being aware and being sensitive to what one is aware of? First of all, it requires the capacity to be puzzled. Children still have the capacity to be puzzled. But once they are through the process of education, most people lose the capacity of wondering, of being surprised. They feel they ought to know everything, and hence that it is a sign of ignorance to be surprised or puzzled by anything."

Erich Fromm

"Age 7—Why? Age 17— Why not? Age 37— Because."
David Campbell

Where Most Ideas Come From

Nothing in here

If you don't know anything, it's going to be hard for you to do anything with your knowledge! If nothing goes in, nothing will be able to come out. On the other hand, **the more information you have to work with, the more connections you have the potential of making.**

Nothing out here

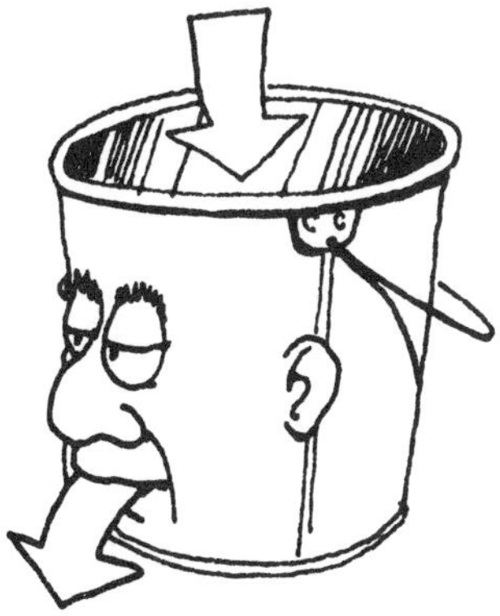

You can't drink from an empty bucket.

You can't create from an empty head.

New creative ideas are usually combinations of existing ideas. The more existing ideas you have in your head, the more connections you'll be able to make. And thus the more creative you'll be able to be.

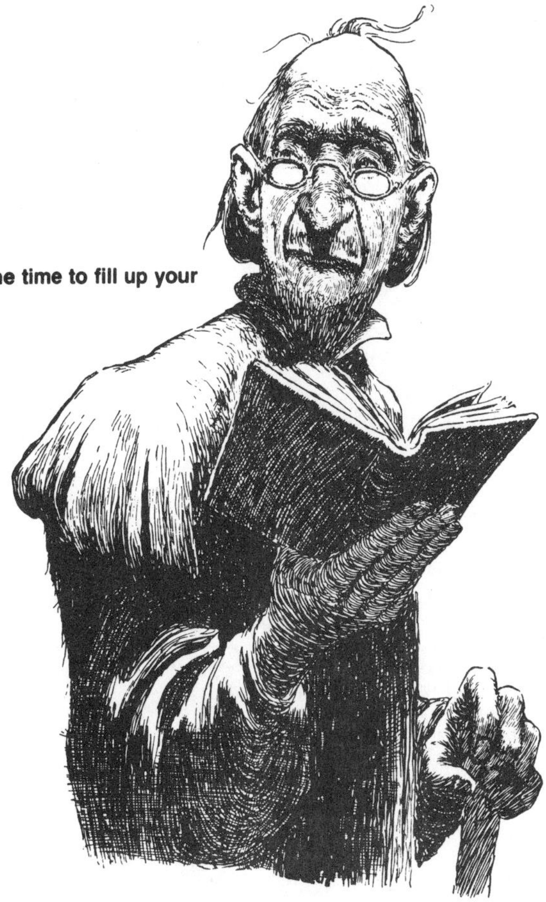

Take the time to fill up your mind.

I used to teach a class in creativity at a major university. I noticed there were two kinds of students: the wingers and the searchers.

The wingers had natural ability, and they'd just sit there and "wing it." They'd rely on their native ability to help them get solutions to the problems I gave them. And they did good work.

The searchers also had native ability. But they wouldn't rely only on their own abilities. They'd also go out and work and search and get other ideas. And whereas the wingers only did good work, the searchers did *outstanding* work. Both as a group and as individuals, they consistently outdid the wingers.

77

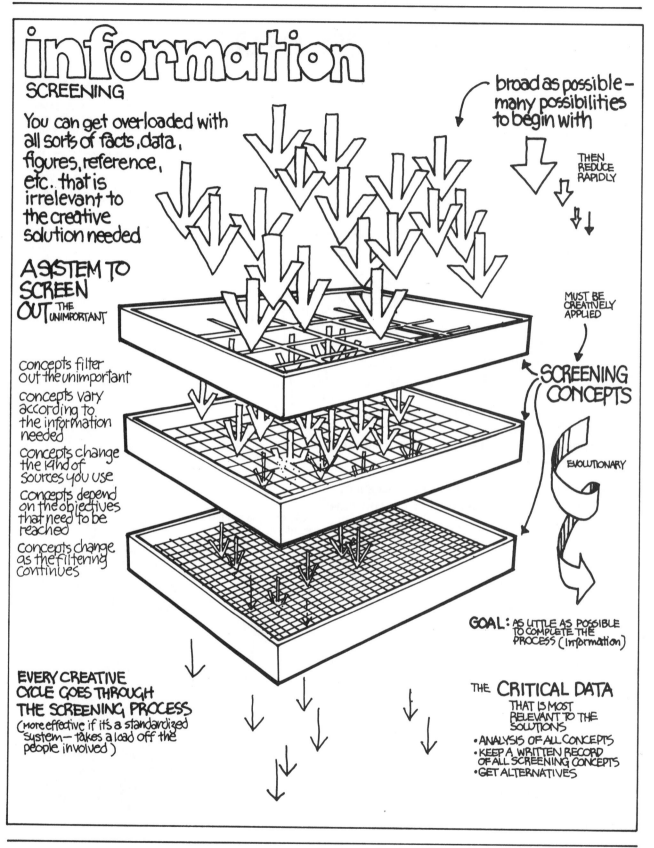

information

SCREENING

You can get overloaded with all sorts of facts, data, figures, reference, etc. that is irrelevant to the creative solution needed

A SYSTEM TO SCREEN OUT THE UNIMPORTANT

concepts filter out the unimportant

concepts vary according to the information needed

concepts change the kind of sources you use

concepts depend on the objectives that need to be reached

concepts change as the filtering continues

broad as possible — many possibilities to begin with

THEN REDUCE RAPIDLY

MUST BE CREATIVELY APPLIED

SCREENING CONCEPTS

EVOLUTIONARY

GOAL: AS LITTLE AS POSSIBLE TO COMPLETE THE PROCESS (information)

EVERY CREATIVE CYCLE GOES THROUGH THE SCREENING PROCESS
(more effective if it's a standardized system — takes a load off the people involved)

THE CRITICAL DATA
THAT IS MOST RELEVANT TO THE SOLUTIONS
- ANALYSIS OF ALL CONCEPTS
- KEEP A WRITTEN RECORD OF ALL SCREENING CONCEPTS
- GET ALTERNATIVES

Here is a technique that will help you to filter out information and overcome the problem of overload.

The Most Important Creative Skill

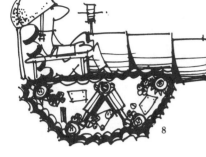

Questions act like bombshells: they open up people and problems. By shooting questions at a problem, a person goes on the offensive, making the problem give up its own solutions.

The ability to ask questions is the most important of all creative skills. When you don't ask questions, nothing happens. If you ask the wrong questions, things happen wrong. But when you ask questions, and they're the right ones, suddenly you've opened the door to your solutions.

"To seek the answers to these questions and discover the further questions which these answers raise, we must search for that which we do not know . . . and that type of search we call CREATIVITY."

Major Marjorie Menebee

Consider what Susanne Langer has said: "The treatment of a problem begins with its first expression as a question. The way a question is asked limits the ways in which any answer to it may be given. A question is merely an ambiguous proposition; the answer is its determination."

The Question Gives the Answer

And answers to one question can often answer questions you didn't think to ask. Newton's questions about why objects fall to the ground led to answers about why planets orbit the sun—and these answers eventually let us send men to the moon and machines to Mars.

Ray Bradbury said, "Each man that asks questions beyond his own time must face questions where there are no proven answers." Sometimes our questions will not be totally answerable. Yet the simple fact that we've asked them will make the difference to the creativity. The question will open our minds and help us to see some of the possible solutions to our problem.

Not just any question will do. The question must home in on the crux of the problem. It must help the asker identify where to go next. It needs to show the important relationships between the different aspects of the problem.

Good Key Words to Include in Questions:

Who?	**Why?**	**How?**
What?	**When?**	**So What?**
Where?	**Which?**	

And after you've asked those questions, there's one more, to help you see what you've learned:
Well?

Oftentimes, finding the right solution to a problem may be as simple as asking the right question.

Visual Brainstorming

The following is a visual brainstorming session to develop new uses for plastic bubble sheets.

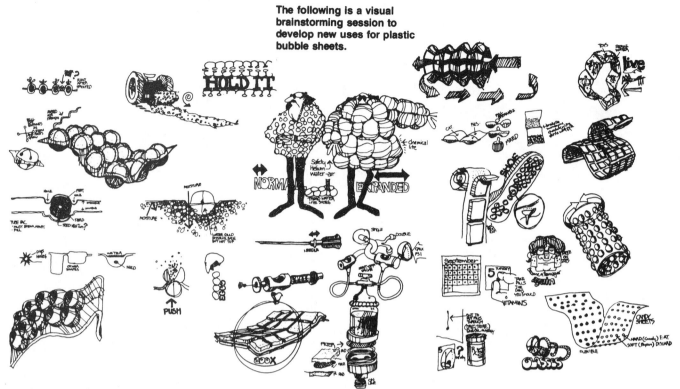

One great way to develop creative ideas is to do a little visual brainstorming. In visual brainstorming, you put your ideas down on pieces of paper, drawing them out as you think. **Visual brainstorming takes ideas from your head and puts them into concrete form.** It makes the difference between vague notions floating somewhere up there in your mind and truly creative ideas that can be used.

Visual brainstorming has benefits you won't get elsewhere:

- It helps you validate your thoughts.
- It helps you see the gaps in your thinking.
- It makes things tangible, brings ideas out into the open where you can more effectively deal with them.

Here are the rules for visual brainstorming:

1. Use large sheets of paper, so you won't feel cramped in.
2. Draw out the ideas as they come to you.
3. Don't make any judgments—just draw.
4. Let your mind make connections from one idea to the next, and draw your connections.
5. When you're finished, look back over what you've done. At this point you can start to make judgments about what works best for your problem.

Using Visual Forms

Visual brainstorming can be done individually or in a group. If you do it in a group, the same rules apply, although one person will generally perform the drawing function for all.

If you're not good at drawing, don't worry. The idea is simply to get your thoughts into a visual form. If it's rough, fine. You've still got *something* to look at!

A visualization of the concepts
of expansion and contraction
in the hopes of finding a new
manufacturing process.

A group of people worked on the same sheet of paper as a creative exercise.

ARROWS

PIERCED ARROW

LIGHTER T

NO

JAUT.

SCHOOL OF ARROWS

ARROW NAUTICAL.

ARROW PARISIAN

ARROWSOL.

SPRAY ARROW

(SP)ARROW HAWK

LIGHTER THAN ARROW.

ARROWS

CUSTER'S LAST STAND

ARROW SHIRT

How Intuition Can Increase Your Creative Potential

We've all had experience with hunches. We get an idea inside us that feels right—and we have a real urge to pursue it. **That's intuition—the feeling that an idea will work even though it has little logical support.**

Nowadays logic and proof are popular, and people often shove off their inward intuitions. But hunches and intuition are still valid. They can make the difference between a truly creative idea and one that's just old and trite.

R. Buckminster Fuller, developer of the geodesic dome (among other things), believes in hunches. "I call intuition cosmic fishing," he said. "You feel a nibble, then you've got to hook the fish." But many of us don't bother to pull the fish in. We shake it out of our heads and light up another cigarette.

Success Through Intuition

Dr. Jonas Salk, who discovered the polio vaccine, was able to make that discovery through an intuitive leap. "Intuition is something we don't understand the biology of yet," he said. "But it is always with excitement that I wake up in the morning wondering what my intuition will toss up to me, like gifts from the sea. I work with it, and rely upon it. It's my partner."

Helen Gurley Brown, editor of *Cosmopolitan*, relies on intuition to help her make the right decisions. "When I read a manuscript, even if it's not well written, only intuition can say this is truth, readers will like it. Or intuition may tell me that a piece by a Pulitzer prize winner is phony."

After Edwin Land invented the Polaroid camera, he faced the incredible challenge of convincing others that it was marketable. Land's contacts told him that his camera was too expensive to be a toy, and yet not refined enough in terms of picture quality to be a fine camera. But Land felt "in his bones" that the camera had tremendous sales potential. He stuck to his intuition until finally it paid off big.

Creative Intuition Can Be Increased By Using These Three Helps

Our hunches can make all the difference between being creative and becoming stale. To make them work for you, do three things:

1. **Refuse to discard hunches.** They may seem silly or worthless—yet they *could* prove to be invaluable.

2. **Check them out.** When intuition comes to you, try it out to see if it's a crazy idea or a brilliant one.

3. **Cultivate intuition.** Let your subconscious mind help you out on problems. When you're stumped, turn the problem over to the subconscious to work on for a while. When the answer comes back, it may seem to be "just a hunch." But be sure to listen to it.

"Intuitive thinking, the training of hunches, is a much neglected and essential feature of productive thinking."

Jerome Bruner

Swimming Upstream

"It takes courage to be creative, just as soon as you have a new idea, you're in the minority of one."

E. Paul Torrance

The only way to create an idea and not have this problem is to live all alone on a Pacific island.

Even then to get off the island you will have to start swimming.

You put on your swimming suit and go to the river. You jump in and start to swim. You're a good swimmer and have good form. Yet you aren't getting anywhere. All day and all night you swim, stroking away. Finally, exhausted, you crawl to the bank—the same bank you started from.

It's tough to get anywhere when you're swimming upstream.

Whenever a person comes up with a new idea, he should expect that it will be met with resistance. **Unique ideas are always resisted. Trying to bring them to reality can be as difficult as swimming upstream.**

That doesn't mean that you should give up. If you believe in your idea, go for it. *But know that there will be resistance.*

impatience
uniformity
fear of ridicule
conceit
no funding
confusion
insecurity
jealousy
group thinking
laziness
apathy
lack of commitment
intolerance
tenseness
fear of change

tradition
control
overspecialization
negativism
prejudice
fear of failure

You with your idea →

"The man with a new idea is a crank until the idea succeeds."

Mark Twain

"One of the greatest pains to human nature is the pain of a new idea."

Walter Bagehot

The Biggest Barrier to Creativity

Creative people often have fears. It doesn't matter how well things have gone in the past, there's always a little voice inside that makes some people doubt their creative work. With that voice they tell themselves:

"I may fail this time."

"It's been quite a while since I had a good creative idea. I've probably lost my touch."

"I'm too shy to really be able to move ahead."

"I may lose all my money."

"I may ruin my reputation."

"I'm afraid of what others will say or think."

"It probably won't work anyway."

"It may all turn out to be a mistake."

Fear is one of the biggest barriers to creativity. It locks the mind up and won't let it function. It freezes things into position and won't let them move.

Yet the fear is also the sign of a creative mind. The person who becomes afraid of things that don't yet exist (and probably never will) is showing the power of his imagination. His mind is obviously strongly creative!

The only problem is that the person's creative abilities are turned in the wrong direction—into worries instead of solutions. He needs to turn the negative images into positive ones. He needs to rechannel his thoughts in another direction.

If you have strong fears, you know you have a good imagination! It's just incorrectly applied.

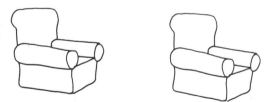

A strong fear is simply a good imagination wrongly directed. Turn your imagination from fears to positive thinking, and you'll be able to develop a creative solution to your problem.

A Noncreative Habit to Avoid

Margaret Samuelson always cut off both ends of the ham before she stuck it in the oven to roast. Her husband, Ross, was curious. "Why in the world do you do that?" he asked her one day.

"I don't know!" Margaret answered, looking surprised at herself. "That's just the way my mom always did it."

That Thanksgiving Margaret's family had a big reunion at her grandmother's house. Ross saw his big chance. He cornered his mother-in-law. "Margaret cuts the ends off the ham before she cooks it. But she doesn't know why—she just says you taught her. What is the reason?"

"I really don't know," came the answer. "My mom just taught me to do it that way."

Ross was getting more and more curious. The first chance he got, he sat down with Grandma and asked his question. "Is it part of your religious custom, or does the ham cook better that way, or what?"

Grandma laughed. "Nothing like that at all!" she answered. "When I was first married, we had a tiny oven. The only way the ham would fit was to cut off both ends. I guess I never got out of the habit!"

Often we get stuck in our ruts of habit without even thinking of it. The way it happens is easy: **Roads too often traveled turn into ruts.** It happens slowly and easily. We're so comfortable while it's happening we don't even notice.

Then, all of a sudden, when we do notice, it's too late to change. We're *stuck!* And that's where the problem comes. When people get into ruts, it's hard to change directions. It happens to individuals, organizations, countries, companies, schools, churches, everyone!

When we're in a rut, it's hard to be creative. In fact, habitual ruts and creativity are literally enemies!

"Rut: A grave with both ends open."

Stay in the same path too long and you'll end up in a rut.

Pushed Out of the Rut

To get out of a rut and back into a creative lifestyle usually requires some force. An *external force* can do the job. Water rushing down the rut after you, a flash flood, can motivate you to get out of the rut very quickly!

Back in the early days of the motion-picture industry, things were going well for most companies. People were going to the movies in droves, and the money was rolling in for the production companies. When the technology for producing "talkies" was refined, company after company turned it down. *Why mess with success?*

they reasoned. They were settled deeply and comfortably in their ruts.

But there was an exception. Warner Brothers was having serious financial times, and bankruptcy loomed. Their financial troubles forced them out of their rut—when they had an opportunity to produce a talkie, they grabbed at it. It not only saved their financial skins, but for many years thereafter Warner Brothers was at the top of the Hollywood heap.

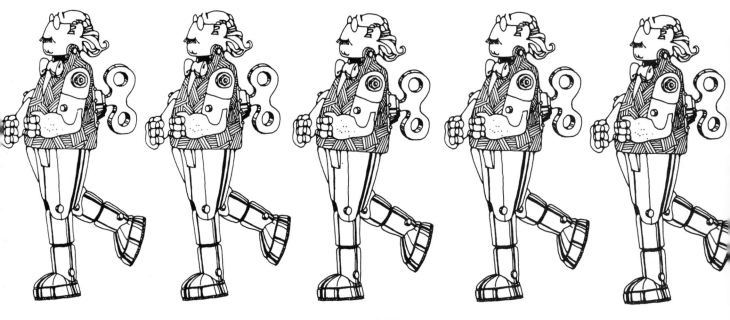

A Healthy Injection

If no external force comes along to push you out of the rut, you may need to find something *internal* to make it happen. The best thing I've found is to inject something new:

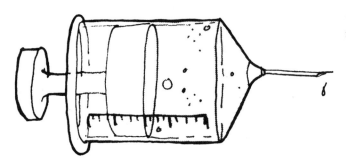

Injecting something new into your life and work can help you out of a rut.

- Take a new route to and from work. I realized how deeply ingrained my traveling routine was one day when I arrived home from work—and didn't even remember making the trip! I started to inject something new into my routine by taking another route, and then still another one.

- Try something different. One small change can revolutionize your thinking. One man took a second job as a night cook once a week. It made him a little extra money, and at the same time it helped him gain new points of view.

- Study and try to understand a totally new subject.

- Make a new friend, someone whose lifestyle and way of thinking are different from yours.

- Go somewhere you've never been before—somewhere you wouldn't normally go.

- If worse comes to worst, make the BIG changes: one friend has moved eight times and changed jobs five times, all in an effort (successful, happy) to keep his thinking fresh. His example is probaly extreme, but sometimes big changes are necessary.

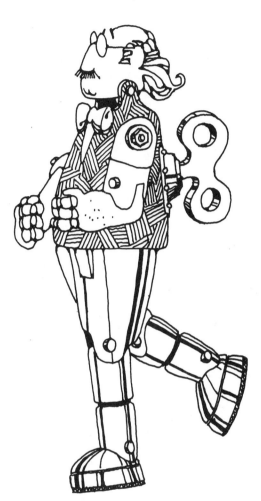

The last people to see they are in a rut are the people already in it.

"Two roads diverged in a wood, and I— I took the one less traveled by, And that has made all the difference."

Robert Frost

Pointy-Headed People Need Custom-Made Hats

A standard-sized hat doesn't cover a pointed head very well.

Often creative people need peculiar things to help them in their work. Their need may seem absurd. But if the creator thinks it's necessary, give him what he needs. If he thinks it will help, he's probably right. If nothing else, giving the creator what he needs may be the start of a self-fulfilling prophecy.

What if you're the creator, and you get this hare-brained idea? Give yourself what you need! It will probably help. Pointy-headed people need custom-made hats. Creative people are a little bit different from other people. They need things that are different.

"Some of the stimuli with which certain great thinkers sought to surround themselves are curious and even bizarre: yet their presence seems to have been strangely necessary to creative thought. . . . Dr. Johnson needed to have a purring cat, orange peel, and plenty of tea to drink. . . . Zola pulled down the blinds at midday because he found more stimulus for his thought in artificial light. Carlyle was forever trying to construct a soundproof room while Proust achieved one. Schiller seems to have depended on the smell of decomposing apples which he habitually kept concealed in his desk."

P. McKellar, *Imagination and Thinking,* Basic Books

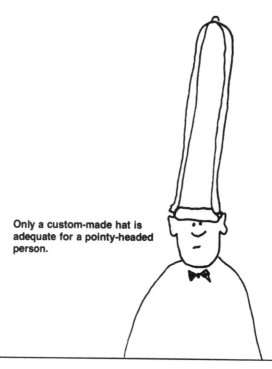

Only a custom-made hat is adequate for a pointy-headed person.

How to Avoid a Creator's Worst Enemy

You've been working on your pet idea for a long time. It started as a fleeting idea in the head. Now it's well developed. You think it's ready to sell to others.

STOP!

Before you take another step, stand back from the idea to get a clearer look at it.

Are you so enchanted with or so close to your idea and the wealth you think it will bring that you can't see its weaknesses?

It's common for people to become so enamored with their ideas that they overlook glaring problems. It's a pitfall that's difficult to avoid, unless the creator consciously takes pains to avoid it. Before you get to the point of investing huge amounts of time and/or money, stand back, take a rest, and carefully, step by step, analyze the idea.

If you need to shelve the idea for a while so you can be more objective, do so.

If you need to seek the input and advice of others, do so.

Do whatever is necessary to evaluate your idea carefully and thoroughly.

Don't lose time by setting the idea aside for too long. But don't waste precious time and money on an ill-conceived idea, either.

A memo from the Superintendent of Patents

Hold your idea too close and you'll fail to see its weaknesses.

emphasizes the need to reconsider carefully before proceeding with an idea:

"Patents are frequently taken out for the most trifling inventions or improvements. The treasury fee is $30; and many patents, when obtained, are not worth as many cents. Yet, the applicant is highly offended if advised to keep his money."

This device was actually patented. It tipped the hat of a gentleman when a lady passed by. Would you buy it? Can you see why it failed?

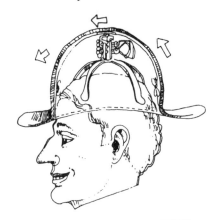

Creative Cliches

Tyrannical Director

Moody Poet

Temperamental Writer

Flashy Designer

The ability to be creative is not confined to any one group or type of person. Anyone, in any kind of endeavor, can be creative. All that's required is the *desire* to make it happen, and the *willingness* to expend the necessary effort.

Because this is true, we should take care not to jump to conclusions, either about ourselves or about others. It takes more to be creative than to simply fit a cliche. At the same time many people fit the cliche because they are creative!

See if you recognize yourself—or someone you know.

What do these cliches mean?

First, that any personality-type can be creative. No matter who a person is or what he looks like or what his eccentricities are, he can be creative. If he is willing to get busy.

Second, that surface appearance doesn't mean a thing. Creativity is inside, not outside. Anyone who wishes to be creative must change the inner person.

Wiz Kid

Absentminded Professor

"All men are born with a very definite potential for creative activity."

John E. Arnold

Eccentric Inventor

Starving Artist

Tips for Dealing With the Right People

People can be a tremendous help or a gigantic bother. You'll need to work with other people to get your idea completed. They can provide financing, marketing, and technical assistance in ways you couldn't yourself. Your ability to work effectively with others will greatly influence the speed and quality with which your idea grows to completion. Be prepared to protect yourself as you rely on the assistance of others.

Probably the most important thing to do as you work with others is this: **Know who you are dealing with. The more you know about others—especially if you know the right things—the greater security you'll have in working with them. And the greater your ultimate chance of success will be.**

It's nice to believe that the other guy is completely trustworthy, that he will do what he says, but that too often is not the case. A few minutes spent checking out the other person can save a lot of future grief.

Talk to Others

Talk to people who have worked with this person before—employers, employees, subcontractors, partners. What is his track record? What are his previous successes and failures? What has he done or not done in the past that might influence your decision to work with him? Don't be satisfied with just one or two sources. Check as many as you can. An ounce of prevention is worth a pound of cure.

The Missing Ingredient

Stephen, a high school shop teacher, had a good idea. He devised an instructional teaching kit that made the teacher's job easier. He tried the kits out on his students, and they loved them. Some of his colleagues tried the kits, and their response was enthusiastic. Stephen knew he had a winner.

Initial marketing tests proved he was right. He had something that could make him rich. The frosting on the cake came when Stephen received an offer from a well-respected distributing company that wanted to buy the rights to Stephen's kits. The company had a good name, and Stephen didn't feel he needed to check them out. He sold the rights to the kits for a small advance, glorying in the thought of the big money the company promised he would receive later.

The success quickly turned sour when Stephen learned that the company was having financial problems. They had overextended themselves; they had let their inventory get too large; and it soon became apparent that they wouldn't be able to invest the necessary capital to make the kits big sellers. Stephen is still waiting for that big money.

Some people are all promises and no follow-through. Some are all take and no give.

When you check other people out, look primarily for two things:

Are they honest?
Are they competent?

You can lose your idea, and its rewards, if others fail to measure up in either respect. A klutz can lose the idea for you, and a crook can take it from you.

The People Checker

A tendency of many creators is to involve too many people. You know a brother-in-law who can help. Then there's a friend from high school. Your neighbor told you about this superb salesman—and on it goes. Soon you find yourself overloaded to the point that you've got to get rid of some of your "helpers" to even get the idea off the ground.

The answer to the problem of getting overloaded—or underloaded—is to use a People Checker. I've provided one below. By filling out a People Checker on every person you think you

might like to use, you'll be able to better evaluate their strengths and weaknesses. And you'll know better if you want them on your team.

At first you should actually fill the People Checker out with pen or pencil. But as you become more accustomed to evaluating others objectively, you'll be able to do much of the task mentally. As you read through the People Checker, think about your own situation; you may think of a few items that you should add to the checklist.

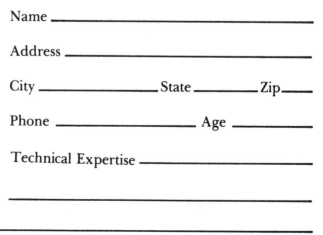

Name _____

Address _____

City _____ State _____ Zip _____

Phone _____ Age _____

Technical Expertise _____

_____

Other Pertinent Information

_____

_____

_____

Objectivity

When you are evaluating another person, it is essential that you be objective in your evaluation. You should not allow prejudices (such as family ties) or emotional involvement (such as friendship) color your appraisal of the individual. You must be able to take a cold, hard look at the person to determine his or her worth to your success.

How did you become acquainted? _____

_____

Do you feel pressured to involve this person?

_____

Are you related? _____

Are you in any way emotionally involved with the

person? _____

Other _____

_____

Purpose

Only two reasons exist for you to involve other people in your project: (1) they can offer financial assistance; (2) they can offer needed technical assistance, such as knowledge or skills.

Why do you need this person? _____

_____

Can you find the same help elsewhere? _____

Where? _____

Can it be done better by someone else? _____

Who? _____

Can another person help for less cost to you?

_____

Who? _____

Other _____

_____

Capability

Is the person you are evaluating *capable* of doing the work that you need done? You will have to determine this by carefully evaluating the person and by checking as many sources as possible to obtain or to verify information about the individual. It can be very discouraging to find that someone you rely on can't do the job. And it can create many problems down the road as well.

What are the past successes of the individual?

_____

_____

What are his or her special skills or capabilities?

_____

_____

Why is the person helping you? _____

_____

_____

Is he stable? _____

How long has he been at this business? _____

_____

What is his financial status? _____

_____

Is this person well respected in his area of

expertise? _____

General Information

When you are seeking someone else to help you with your idea, you should also consider his *integrity, the security of your idea,* and *his level of commitment.* Check a few references to learn other people's appraisal of the person. Ask questions to determine the following kinds of information:

Is the person honest? _____

Does he pay bills on time? _____

Would the person used as reference employ the.

person in this kind of task? _____

Is your idea safe with the person? _____

Is the person responsible? Does he do what he

says he'll do? _____

Is the person in good physical health? _____

Does he have time for your project? _____

Does he believe in your project? _____

Is he personally committed to seeing your project

succeed? _____

Bank Reference _____

_____

Comments _____

Credit Reference _____

Comments _____

Co-Worker of Former Employee _____

_____

Comments _____

Personal Reference _____

_____

Comments _____

Personal Reference _____

_____

Comments _____

Other _____

Conclusion

What is your final conclusion about the person? Is his value to you and your idea more than the cost in time, money, effort, or worry? If the value is not greater than the anticipated cost, don't involve the person.

Think twice before you start to work with someone else—you don't want to end up with a turkey!

How to Avoid Having Your Idea Stolen

Tie yourself to your idea, so they can't have IT without YOU!

Mike had an idea for a new plant-growing device. He spent a good deal of time and money building a business based on his device. But after two years, Mike discovered he was severely overdrawn. Bills were coming in and he didn't have any money to pay them.

There was only one way out: Mike need to find an investor who could put the needed capital into his fledgling business. He looked around, and sent the word out, and before long just the right investor came along.

Two years have passed. Mike's business is doing better than ever. And Mike's still in charge.

Maintain Control

Mike's being in charge is the best part of all. Large investors are often powerful enough and wealthy enough that once they put their foot in the door they can force out the original owner. But Mike wasn't about to let that happen. He was smart enough to wrap the business so tightly around himself that the business would fail if he were forced out.

The day will come when your idea is ready to take to the marketplace. When you have to work with other people, maintain as much control as you can. Share no more of your idea than is absolutely necessary. Try to tie your idea and yourself into one package, so that one is no good without the other. Fuse what you know and who you are with what you can do with your idea.

The Secret: Tie Your Idea to Yourself

Wayne was an inventor with a lot of talent. But time after time, when he tried to convert his talent into money, he got ripped off. Finally he reached the point where he was afraid to trust others. When he got his next idea, he took on a business partner and had a lawyer draw up a legal agreement between them. "If you help me succeed, you'll succeed too," Wayne said. "But if you allow anyone to take advantage of me, you'll go down the tubes at the same time."

By tying his latest idea so closely to himself, Wayne was finally able to succeed financially. He's now worth hundreds of thousands of dollars, just from that one idea.

If you're the one who knows more about the idea than anyone else, you'll be the one who'll know best how to make it work. You'll be, literally, irreplaceable.

As one venture capitalist says of the creator he's financing: "I really need him and his talents. I'd be absolutely lost if he weren't around. And so would everyone else."

A Fact Everybody Forgets

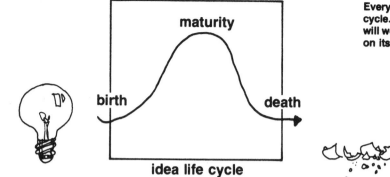

idea life cycle

Every idea has its own life cycle. The successful creator will work with an idea when it's on its way up, not down.

Arnie was a very creative type. One day he came up with an idea that was going to make him rich. That's what he told his friends—and they agreed that it could very well be a marketable idea.

Arnie's idea was simple enough. It involved index cards with holes punched around the borders. By cutting through to the hole according to a prearranged plan, the user could create an automatic filing access system for himself. The idea could be adapted for recipes, school notes, favorite quotes, or a number of other applications.

In essence, Arnie had invented a manual computer. And that was the problem with Arnie's idea. He produced his cards at about the time home computers were beginning to catch on. His cards sold for about 1/1,000th of the cost of a computer, but people couldn't help but compare the two. "This is a good idea," they'd tell him. "Think of how well my computer will do these things when I finally get one."

Arnie's idea never has caught on. But it was the love of his life, and he just won't let it go. People aren't much interested in it. But Arnie is committed to it nonetheless.

Arnie is having a hard time accepting a sad truth: **Ideas don't last forever.** Every idea on this planet goes through a life cycle: it's born; it matures; it dies. The problem comes when the creator clings to the idea even after it's dead.

- Dorothy Rodgers, wife of composer Richard Rodgers, hated to clean with old-fashioned rag mops. One day she came up with a better idea: a mop with a disposable swab. For many years she received royalty payments for her idea, which she sold to Johnson and Johnson. But now her patent has expired and the mop doesn't make much money anymore. It would be foolish to continue to push her Johnny Mop.

- An author wrote one book in her life, on her area of expertise, and she made good money off it for many years. But eventually it became outdated, and other books began to replace it in the marketplace. Finally the publisher allowed it to go out of print. The author was furious! She even threatened lawsuit against the books that began to replace hers. She didn't realize that books have a life cycle just like everything else.

- Other examples: hula-hoops! Also, corset pulls, object teaching, pet rocks, hair oil, buggy whips, Davy Crockett hats, fins on cars, quadrophonic sound.

Fit Today's Needs

Surviving and thriving in the idea world depends on coming up with *new* ideas to fit the circumstances of the time. The new idea can simply be a resurrection of an old idea, of course, but in the new context it becomes NEW!

One secret to success in creativity, then: recognize that all ideas have a life cycle. Continually create anew.

Don't Overlook This Technique of Creative Thinking

> "To know one thing, you must know the opposite . . . just as much, else you don't know that one thing. So that, quite often, one does the opposite as an expression of the positive."
>
> Henry Moore

The creative process is often a dynamic oscillation between opposites. To understand the positive, we must know the negative. When we see only one or the other, problems arise. We make judgments based on only half the data. But when we understand both sides of an issue we'll be able to deal with it creatively.

Life is a study in opposites:

birth-death	male-female	win-lose
build-destroy	yin-yang	strong-weak
up-down	laughter-tears	light-dark
love-hate	joy-sorrow	plus-minus

When we know how the opposites interact with one another, we have the information we need to solve the problem. We're able to "see both sides of the issue," which results in greater creativity.

Opposition Leads to Creation

An understanding of opposition gave Einstein a great insight into the relationship between Newtonian physics and his own theory of relativity. Can a thing be in motion and at rest at the same time? The question seems foolish. Yet contemplating the opposites at work in the universe gave Einstein this explanation:

"For an observer in free fall from the roof of a house, there exists, during his fall, no gravitational field . . . in his immediate vicinity. If the observer releases any objects, they will remain, relative to him, in a state of rest. The [falling] observer is therefore justified in considering his state as one of 'rest.' "

For a musician, the points of rest, where there is no sound or music, are as important to the musical piece as are the musical strains.

For a writer, "what you don't say is as important as what you do say."

For an artist, "the negative shape is more important than the positive. Most people don't even see it, but if you get the negative shape right, the positive will almost always be right."

For any creator: Knowing the relationship of the opposites often leads to a creative solution.

> "The sad truth is that man's real life consists of a complex of inexorable opposites—day and night, birth and death, happiness and misery, good and evil. We are not even sure that one will prevail against the other, that good will overcome evil, or joy defeat pain. Life is a battleground. It always has been, and always will be; and if it were not so, existence would come to an end."
>
> Carl Jung

The Yin-Yang symbol gives a visual demonstration of the opposites in life.

> "Under Heaven all can see beauty only as beauty because there is ugliness. All can know good as good only because there is evil."
>
> Lao-tzu

How to Submit an Idea

Don't just send your idea out. Take steps first to protect it from greedy hands.

Eventually the day will come when most creative people want to submit their idea to a manufacturer or producer. The time has arrived to get the idea going in the marketplace. But don't just jump in and send your creation out. There's another important step you must take first.

The crucial thing to do at this point is to **contact the company initially before you send them anything.** The approach is simple: send them a letter describing what you're up to, in very general terms. Then wait for their reply.

The company's response accomplishes two important things:

First, it turns the tables, so that now you're sending your idea *at the company's invitation.* That makes a difference in terms of legal protection as well as how well the company will receive the idea.

Second, it will give you a written record, on the company's letterhead, of when the company was first made aware of you and your idea.

A Sample Letter

The letter you send can be short and to the point. Here's a sample of what the letter could contain:

New Products Division
XYZ Manufacturing Co.
Wherever, USA 01010

Gentlemen:

I have invented a new product (or . . . I have an idea for a new product) that I feel would fit right into your product line.

The product is . . . (here put a brief but clear description of what it is you wish to submit, what you think the marketing potential is, and so forth. *But don't go into enough detail to give it all away.*)

I would like to submit this product for your examination and consideration. Please send me whatever release forms or other material your company requires for such submissions.

Sincerely,

Your Name

Constipated Thinking

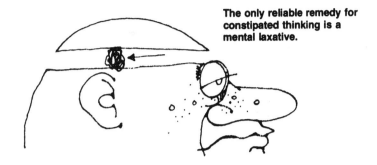

The only reliable remedy for constipated thinking is a mental laxative.

Listen to these typical people with a typical problem:

> "Mrs. Yates, my English teacher, gave me this theme to do. I'm supposed to have it done by tomorrow to read in front of my whole class. I've tried and tried, but I'm not making any headway on it. I write a page, then have to tear it up because it doesn't make any sense."

> "I've been working on this same painting for three weeks now. One look will tell you how far I've gotten on it: nowhere! I'll get a little painted, but it looks so crummy that I paint over it with white to start again."

> "My children are real brats! I want to help them learn how to do better, but I just can't get any ideas. I've read all the books, but when I try to apply them, they don't work with my kids."

> "My employees need to work harder. I need to get production up. But I don't know how. I've wrestled with the problem for months now. But nothing seems to come."

> "I'm working on this invention, but it isn't going anywhere. Nothing I try will work. I don't know if the problem is me or the invention. Maybe I'm trying to do something that's impossible."

Typical people with typical problems. **The more a person gets stuck in one way of thinking, the less he's able to think of new ways to resolve his problem.** The way of thinking can be emotional, intellectual, social, or physical. These can put up barriers to other routes of approaching a problem, cutting off new solutions and creative ideas.

There's a scientific name for this problem. It's called *constipated thinking,* where you get mentally stuck for new ideas, for solutions to problems.

Getting Unstuck

The best remedy for constipated thinking is to take a *mental laxative.* Here are the ways to take the laxative:

- **Sit on it.** Put the problem away and think of something else. Get a change of scenery. Find something else to do. Let time work for you. If you try to force things when you're stuck, you'll often get stuck worse. But put it aside and you'll start to get results.

- **Review your goal.** It often helps to take a second look at *why* you're trying to solve the problem. Review your motives, your reasons for working on the problem. Sometimes people get stuck because they've lost sight of their goal and have wandered off on the wrong track.

- **Get some exercise.** The human animal is a unique creature. It needs development both mentally and physically. If you've become unbalanced on one side or the other, get some exercise. Don't allow either your intellect or your physical muscles to atrophy. When a person gets stuck on a problem, he may have been neglecting part of his overall being. The creative person is by necessity a complete person.

- **Get new input.** We often get too close to ourselves and our problems. We get too attached to the problem we're working on to see it objectively. When we get constipated, we can have someone who has no vested interest take a look at the problem. At the same time, it may help to look for a solution in other fields. Someone in another discipline may have solved a related problem you can then transfer to your needs.

Sometimes the little things can get you stopped up completely.

Here's something that will help you remove the blockages in your thinking.

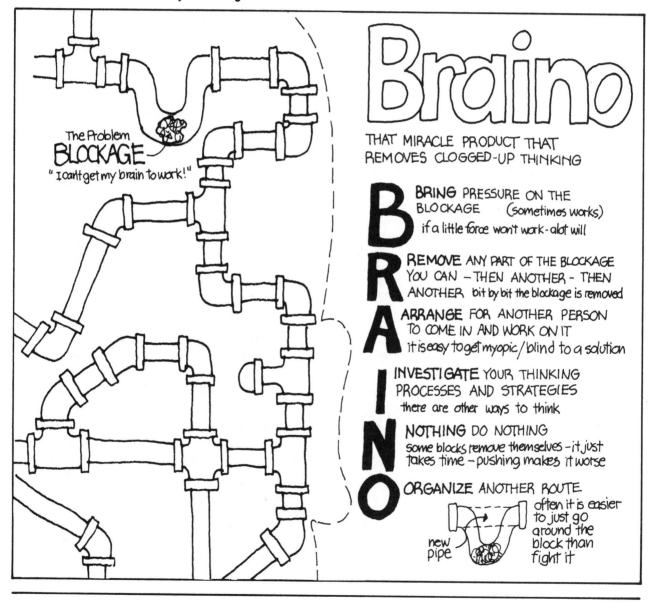

The Problem
BLOCKAGE
"I can't get my brain to work!"

Braino

THAT MIRACLE PRODUCT THAT REMOVES CLOGGED-UP THINKING

BRING PRESSURE ON THE BLOCKAGE   (sometimes works)
if a little force won't work - a lot will

REMOVE ANY PART OF THE BLOCKAGE YOU CAN — THEN ANOTHER — THEN ANOTHER bit by bit the blockage is removed

ARRANGE FOR ANOTHER PERSON TO COME IN AND WORK ON IT
it is easy to get myopic/blind to a solution

INVESTIGATE YOUR THINKING PROCESSES AND STRATEGIES
there are other ways to think

NOTHING DO NOTHING
some blocks remove themselves - it just takes time - pushing makes it worse

ORGANIZE ANOTHER ROUTE
often it is easier to just go around the block than fight it
new pipe

How to Increase Creative Output Without Extra Work

We each have a time when we are the most productive. Some people are night owls. Others are early birds. Everyone's internal clock is different. The closer we can align our work time with our productive time, the greater results we'll have. If we can do our creative work during our productive time, we'll end up with more creative results.

Willard had a real problem with his internal clock. He let the expectations of society determine his daily schedule. He worked an eight-to-five job—but his mind and body were out-of-sync then. His most productive time was in the early morning hours.

For years Willard struggled along. He'd work his eight-to-five, then he'd go home. He'd piddle away the evening hours. Late in the evening, he'd go to bed, just like everyone around him. But then, around two a.m., he'd wake up. His mind would be racing with ideas. He'd write them down. But he never had any creative time to work on their implementation.

Willard will probably finish his life the way he started it: out-of-sync. He'll end without making the creative contribution he'd like to. It doesn't have to be that way. He *could* get on a different work schedule, one that would accommodate his internal clock.

Find Your Best Time

The conflict comes when our environment and our internal rhythm don't match. The internal

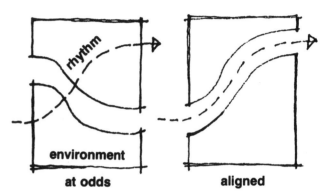

When we align our work time (environment) with our time of productivity (rhythm), creativity will increase.

at odds **aligned**

clock ticks away, and we don't get the benefit from our potentially most productive times.

> "I work best in the very early hours, from four to six a.m."

> "My most effective time is around eleven o'clock at night."

> "I'm lucky. I work from nine-to-five, and from nine to noon is my best time."

There's a way for each of us to find our most productive time. First, think of your past experiences. What times were most rewarding? Identify the times and circumstances that went with creative experiences.

Second, repeat those experiences. Recreate the circumstances, at the same times. For example, if you're most productive from four to six a.m., arrange your life so you can use those hours on a regular basis, say one morning a week, or twice a month. The rewards will make any fatigue you occasionally suffer well worth it.

Do YOU Do It?

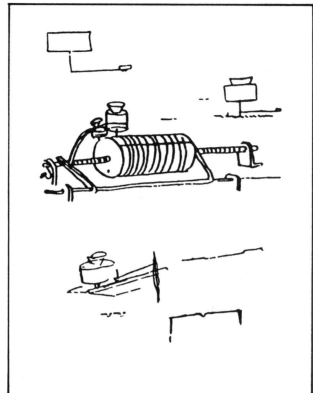

Edison's sketch of his idea for a phonograph, taken from his notebook.

Inventors do it! Writers do it! Artists do it!

Creative people of all persuasions do it!

And what is it that they do? **They keep a notebook or journal to record their ideas.**

Einstein commonly wrote down his thoughts. Edison sketched ideas out in detail. Da Vinci's notebooks are famous.

Lost in the Night

Maybe you've shared this experience: It's the middle of the night. You wake up after a dream. You get up to get a drink of water. An idea from the dream suddenly hits you. "That's incredible!", you think. "That will really make a difference with that problem I've been struggling with. In the morning I'll detail it all out on paper."

You climb back in bed and go to sleep. Morning comes. "Ah, yes!" you say. "I remember last night I had this brilliant idea. Now what was it about?"

Unfortunately, the idea is gone. The night's sleep swept it away, back into the darker recesses of your mind.

The only safe and sure way to retain ideas is to write them down. Any other approach is playing with failure.

"Ideas, especially the really good ones, are fragile evanescent things. They flit into the mind at moments of leisure—while bathing, taking a walk, lying in a hammock, driving to work—and they stun us with their brilliance, with their perfection. They are like one of nature's creatures, perfect in coloration and form. But they are just as wary, too. They can vanish as quickly as they came, to disappear into the incredible and labyrinthine forest of the mind. And they can become inextricably lost, never to be seen again."

Author unknown

"A man would do well to carry a pencil in his pocket, and write down the thoughts of the moment. Those that come unsought for are commonly the most valuable, and should be secured, because they seldom return."

Francis Bacon

Finding the Essence

Only by knowing the real problem can you ever find a solution. Go back into the core of the problem as far as you can, stripping away all the useless, redundant, or superfluous ideas about it. You won't be able to do productive work on solving the problem until you've found its essence.

Defining a problem is like shooting at a bull's-eye target. Once you've spotted the target, you know what the basic problem is. But you have to keep shooting at it, trying to hit the exact bull's-eye, before you'll be able to really get at the essence of it.

Unless you've had a lot of practice, you won't be able to hit the bull's-eye on the first try. You'll probably have to shoot several times as you try to zero in. But each shot will help you see where you are, and it will help you get closer on the next shot.

Ducks

A park ranger once had a real problem with people speeding at a camping and museum center. His solution: put "speed bumps" as people entered and left the area. But his solution didn't really work, because the visitors simply sped up again after crossing a bump.

So he decided to strip the problem back to its essence. "Why do people speed?" he wondered. The reason, he decided, was that they wanted to get to where the action was. They were at the park to see new things—and the camping site wasn't one of them.

By finding the real essence of the problem, the park ranger was able to find the real solution: he brought in beautiful, tame ground birds that roamed about the park and roadways. Suddenly the campsite and museum area became a roadside attraction, and people slowed to a safe speed as they tried to get a better look at the birds and not run over them.

When you get sick, you go to a doctor, and he asks all about the symptoms of your problem. By finding out all he can about the symptoms, he's finally able to diagnose the disease.

Make a Diagnosis

The same thing happens when we try to find the essence of any problem we may have. By defining all we can about it, by finding out what the *real* problem is, we're much more able to find the real solution.

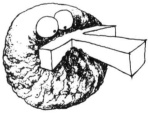

Go back into the problem as far as possible.

Then, once you know the real problem, state it as clearly as possible. That's the first step to meaningful action.

"The formulation of a problem is far more often essential than its solution."

Albert Einstein

"A problem well stated is half solved."
John Dewey

Verbal Agreements Don't Protect Ideas

Don't go just by what people say—get it in writing.

The creator invents a new device or comes up with a great new process. He or she visits a producer, who can turn the idea into something tangible. And profitable. What often comes out of such a meeting? A verbal agreement. Verbal agreements are good starting points. But they're horrible ending points.

It's sad how many disagreements arise over verbal agreements. Time has a way of obscuring each person's perception, altering the memory of what was *really* decided on. Putting a few words on paper alleviates a lot of the problem.

Two brothers went into business together. Surely a verbal agreement was all they would need to work from—after all, they were brothers! But Tom thought they'd agreed on one thing, and Chad was thinking something else. It wasn't long before serious problems cropped up. Harsh words were spoken; families were disrupted. The business dissolved, at a great loss to all concerned.

Verbal agreements are often just as legally binding as written agreements. But it's hard to show what was agreed upon unless the agreement is reduced to writing. The process of writing the agreement down clarifies the ideas and enhances the overall communication. Going through that process will be a lifesaver in a legal battle. But, even more importantly, a written agreement will make the entire working relationship much more productive, much less prone to misunderstanding.

How to Get It Down

It's not difficult to translate a verbal agreement into written form. All one need do is write a letter, sign it, and request the other person to make alterations if necessary. If the other party makes no changes, the agreement will stand as you've written it.

Here's a sample you can follow:

Dear Mr./Mrs./Ms. _____,

(You can start off with a chatty-sounding introductory paragraph, but it is not necessary. The letter need not be formal sounding, though. In fact, a letter that is *too* business-like and to the point can sometimes frighten well-intentioned people away. The most important thing is to be honest and sincere—and to show it.)

I'm writing to confirm the agreement we made last (day of week and date). As I understand it, we agreed to the following: (Here make a specific and carefully itemized list of the things agreed to previously.)

1.

2.

3.

If it seems that I've misunderstood any of the agreement, please let me know immediately. Otherwise, I'll proceed as I've outlined above.

Sincerely,

Your Name

Important: Be sure to keep a copy of the letter in your files!

By taking the simple precaution of turning a verbal agreement into a written one, you'll have much greater protection as you turn your creation from idea into reality.

Brainstorming

Brainstorming can be a fertile source of new ideas.

Brainstorming is one of the most effective ways for groups to work together in finding creative solutions. In brainstorming, the people in the group freely exchange ideas to stimulate new concepts in the minds of others. An idea from one person often stimulates wild responses from another, which in turn causes still more creative thought.

Guidelines for Effective Brainstorming

If the rules are followed, brainstorming can help a group come up with some truly creative—and useful—ideas. If the rules are *not* followed, participants will end up feeling it was all a waste of time.

Since we have enough time-wasters in our society as it is, it's vital that any brainstorming session follow these guidelines:

- **Pick a subject or problem that is understood by all involved.** A lot of time can be wasted if people in your group don't know the problem they are trying to solve. Present the necessary background to the group.

- **Write all the ideas and objectives on a chalkboard or large sheet of paper where everyone can see.** Use words, phrases, or pictures—anything that will rapidly capture the essence of the ideas as they flow from the individuals in the group. New and different

relationships between the ideas expressed will cause additional ideas, but only if all the ideas can be seen together.

No "No No's"

- **No "no-no's."** Your goal is ideas, not judgments. By letting your mind run wild, you can eliminate mental blocks to creative solutions. Don't judge what you or anyone else is thinking. If you have an idea, don't say to yourself, "I won't say it because they'll think I'm stupid." And don't squelch someone else's dumb idea, either—it may stop him from participating, and you need his input. Judge the ideas generated in your brainstorming session AFTER, not during the session.

"Almost all really new ideas have a certain aspect of foolishness when they are first produced."

Alfred N. Whitehead

- **Hitchhike** Let each person's thoughts ride along on another's ideas. Sometimes those off-beat and impractical ideas will trigger still other ideas that can be very useful. That ridiculous idea that you don't want to tell could prompt someone else to think of a smart one.

In brainstorming, don't narrow your vision—search all over in your experiences for ideas that relate to the problem. You may find an idea in literature, yesterday's breakfast, or an insect's mating habits. Connect ideas that don't seem to belong together, and they may inspire the perfect solution.

- **Concentrate on quantity not quality.** A great scientist once said, "The only way to get a good idea is to have lots of ideas." Produce as many ideas as possible; then you will have more from which to pick the best. It is easy, after a brainstorming session, to eliminate useless or ridiculous ideas, But it is extremely difficult to "puff-up" a short list of ideas. Without *QUANTITY,* you'll most likely not find the *QUALITY* ideas either.

"The person who is capable of producing a large number of ideas per unit of time, other things being equal, has a greater chance of having significant ideas."
J. P. Guilford

- **Keep it loose.** Nothing can stop good brainstorming more thoroughly than a leader with a Napoleon complex—a person who commands you to perform, who tries to force you to produce good ideas. Keep unnecessary structure out of it. The command "Get good ideas!" will inhibit a group's creativity. What is needed is an open and free environment which gives an incentive for idea production.

- **Last is best.** The last half of a brainstorming session is often the best. It takes the first half to get all the usual responses and habitual solutions out of the say. When these are removed, what is left are new ideas and new ways of looking at the problem.

Brainstorming is one of the most popular of all creative techniques. Individuals and organizations worldwide have adopted "brainstorming" as a major facet of their creative policies. The reason: It works—if it's done right. If you haven't tried brainstorming yet, you're in for a mind-expanding—possibly exhilarating—experience.

"The ability to relate and to connect, sometimes in an odd and yet striking fashion, lies at the very heart of any creative use of the mind, no matter in what field or discipline."
George J. Seidel

Several brains working together can often come up with exciting new ideas.

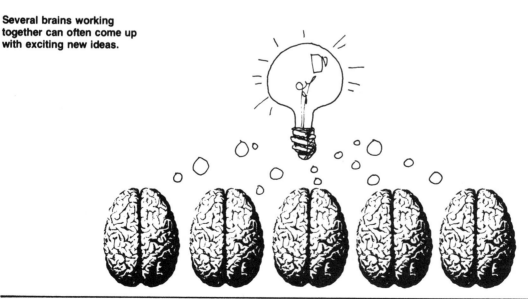

How Ideas Are Stolen

Talk can get you into trouble. Don't talk your success away.

Allen was a natural-born tinkerer. He would spend countless hours tinkering with his projects, devoting all his energies to some invention or another. One day he came up with an exceptional idea—an automated warehouse. He worked out all the details, drawing up blueprints and creating models in his garage. By simply pressing a few buttons, goods in the warehouse could be retrieved and prepared for shipping without human hands.

But Allen made one mistake with his brilliant idea. He forgot to keep it to himself. He told a friend all about it—and the friend took the idea and ran with it. The "friend" has made millions from Allen's automated warehouse idea. Allen didn't make a penny. He's still tinkering in his garage.

Allen teaches us a valuable lesson. **When you get an idea, keep it to yourself as long as possible. Then talk only to those people who really need to know—who can help you advance and protect the idea. The fewer you involve, the better.**

During World War II an old saying became a new slogan on the home front: "Loose lips sink ships." The slogan cautioned against talking about the movements of U.S. ships at the wrong time or place, since such conversations could be overheard by foreign spies who would warn the enemy. A few loose words could effectively fire a submarine torpedo to sink a ship.

Loose Lips Sink Ships

The loose lip problem resulted in thousands of deaths during that war. One example: The Allied forces had determined that it was essential that southern France be invaded to drive out the German occupational forces. Secrecy was a critical element in the invasion. Yet, shortly before the invasion occurred, a German intelligence officer in Rome overheard an American Red Cross worker say, "I've got to get to Naples by August 1. Southern France is going to be invaded in a few weeks." That slight slip of the tongue killed thousands of Allied soldiers.

"Loose lips sink ships." The same principle

applies to your ideas. If you reveal an idea before its time, you can hamper or even destroy its development. Loose lips may cause someone to grab ahold of your idea and sink your ship.

A similar slip of the tongue could kill your idea. Ideas are fragile when they're first formed. A little negative feedback from a close friend could destroy any hope of success. If you are like most people you yearn for encouragement to buoy your spirits. You want someone to get as excited about your idea as you are. Another's positive response will "prove" to your hidden ego that the idea really is worthwhile.

But what if they don't shout "Hurrah!" when you reveal your secret? What if they laugh? Others don't need to steal the idea for their own benefit to make you a loser. Close friends probably won't steal your idea, but because of their own personal insecurities or jealousies, they can be a hindrance to your success. You lose just as much if the idea is not pursued as you would if someone stole the idea from you.

Keep It to Yourself

Be quiet about your thoughts until you have done sufficient research that a little negative (or positive) criticism won't unduly affect your dedication. When you know you have a good idea, talk only to those people who can help you

accomplish your goal. Idle talk can be your worst enemy.

Most of us like to hear ourselves talk. We're forever dreaming of "making it big soon." Ross was no different. He had a plan for making it big, and he liked to talk about it. He had noticed that many fast-food restaurants didn't have a delivery service. He often ordered pizza from a restaurant that delivered. But he couldn't get other foods he wanted, such as chicken or seafood or Chinese food.

"There must be other people, like me, who want something besides pizza," Ross reasoned. "Why don't I work out a deal with restaurants and start a delivery service for hungry people like myself?"

Ross was quite a talker. When he got excited about an idea, he just *had* to share it. So he told an acquaintance about his delivery-service idea.

Now Ross talks about his super idea that's making the other guy rich.

Talk is cheap. But it's action that makes success stories. It hurts to know that *your idea* is helping someone else get to where you want to be.

Loose lips sink ships. Loose lips give away good ideas. Next time you have a good idea, hush up. Keep it to yourself. Use your idea to help you realize *your* fondest dreams, not someone else's.

Don't tell the crocodiles you're crossing the river until you get to the other side.

11

How to Get More Reward for Your Creative Effort

Farmer Smith was always busy, but he never produced.

Farmer Smith loved the earth, and he loved to plant crops. Every spring he planted hundreds of acres of different crops: corn, potatoes, turnips, beets. Through the summer he carefully cultivated to get rid of the weeds and break up the soil; he sprayed for pests and watered the plants just the right amount.

When fall came, and it was time to harvest his crops, Farmer Smith sat on his porch and smiled approvingly at his work. "It's been a good year," he said to his visiting neighbor. "Yes, indeed, a good year. I'm not sure when I've seen such a good bunch of plants."

"But when are you going to harvest them?" the neighbor asked.

"Harvest them? Why should I harvest them? I like them a lot just the way they are!"

Ridiculous as Farmer Smith's attitude seems, he's not the only one who feels that way. Somehow many creative people have developed the false concept that their ideas have merit in and of themselves. Farmer Smith was very successful in coming up with new plants, but he wasn't very successful in taking them to the point where others could use them. In the same way, some creators are great at coming up with ideas, but they don't ever make anything of them.

"Good ideas are a dime a dozen," said William Stevens. "What it takes is someone practical to implement those ideas."

Focus on Returns

What a creative person needs in order to be results-productive as well as idea-productive is the right state of mind. He needs to focus on ends as well as means. **The right kind of results will come only when we focus on the return from an idea, rather than the idea itself.** How long do we have that focus? Until the idea has paid off.

I've known a good number of creative people in my life. And many of them share the same complaint: I don't get any rewards for all my creative work. Why? Because they've put their focus on the creation rather than the results. Once they start emphasizing the end result, rather than just the means, they'll start getting more of the rewards they want.

> "There's an inaccurate characterization of entrepreneurs being full of ideas and flying like bees from one flower to another. That's not how they are. . . . These people have an unusual ability to focus for long periods on one or two important things and exclude the rest."
>
> Burt McMurtry

111

How to Stimulate Creative Thinking

Manipulative verbs are action words that stimulate the mind to create. A person can take the idea he's working on and think of it in terms of the different manipulative verbs—and by doing so, be able to see his ideas in new ways.

Here are some manipulative verbs that can get your mind going:

"A single word, which represents a world of meaning, can get my creative juices going for an entire day."

Alden Perkes
Author

display	size	focus	complement	harden
segregate	hit	distort	hassle	cut
speed-up	subtract	grow	soften	manipulate
eliminate	contrast	mash	reflect	rethink
force	thicken	squeeze	check	retreat
kill	stalk	predict	recheck	reform
transform	relate	secret	concentrate	crack
separate	tighten	build	organize	inflict
multiply	connect	freeze	add	fasten
cycle	define	destroy	repeat	etc.....
subdue	coat	bypass	adapt	
heat	recreate	attract	vibrate	This list could go
detach	release	stimulate	repel	on and on. The
transpose	continue	loosen	hatch	idea is to find the
verbalize	symbolize	lighten	coordinate	right word for
delay	stamp	stretch	extract	the right need
inject	divide	extrude	bury	and work from
flatten	copy	structure	coerce	there.
stimulate	broaden	inflate	enhance	
submerge	attach	deflate	shift	
defend	invert	blur	eat	
bend	unify	search	return	
weigh	insert	rotate	increase	
fluff-up	seduce	visualize	demand	

Partial Picture

If you can only see part of the picture, you may end up in trouble!

Now it's time for a little test. Below you'll find nine dots. It's possible to connect all the dots using four straight lines and without lifting the pencil from the paper. Every dot must have a line through it. You may start now!

```
  •     •     •


  •     •     •


  •     •     •
```

Many people in trying to solve this puzzle find their minds limited by their preconceptions. They work with parallel lines and try to draw their way around the square. That, of course, isn't the correct solution. The only way to solve the puzzle is to take a step back from it and look at it in a completely new way. (You'll see the answer on the next page, in the margin.)

The approach that works in solving the puzzle is also a valuable approach in being creative. **The more completely a person can see a problem, along with all its possibilities, the more effective he'll be in finding a solution.**

Most of the time we face a problem, we bring our own set of preconceptions to it. Each of us has a unique mind-set, with its own parameters—and those parameters limit our creativity. Just as in the example above, we are limited by not allowing ourselves to see the whole picture, to see all the possibilities.

Open the Mind

When we open our minds, though, creative things begin to happen. One power company had a serious problem: Ice formed on their lines every winter. When the cold hit, the ice began to accumulate. And since the weather didn't break for weeks on end, the ice became so heavy that its weight would break the power lines.

The company's response was the obvious one: they sent their men and equipment out to repair the lines. The expense was great, but what else could they do?

One winter some company executives were discussing the problem and began to brainstorm solutions. For the first time, some of them were able to look at the big picture—and for the first time, they came up with some creative solutions.

The winner: "Why don't we fly helicopters over the lines. The downdraft would blow the ice off before it got so heavy."

Too Impractical?

At first glance the idea was impractical. But as the executives examined it further, they realized that it might have merit. They tried it out during the next freeze and discovered that it solved the problem while costing less than their repairs had.

Whenever we're faced with a difficult problem, one good solution is to release the mind from its parameters and to see the whole picture, not just the part we see at first glance.

Here's the answer to the test. Only by looking at the broader context can one solve the problem.

The picture is never clear when you start the creative process. I've had many a creator say, "If I had known what I was getting into and the high costs involved, I don't think I would have started in the first place." I think they would have done it anyway. The process itself is the most rewarding part of the creative process.

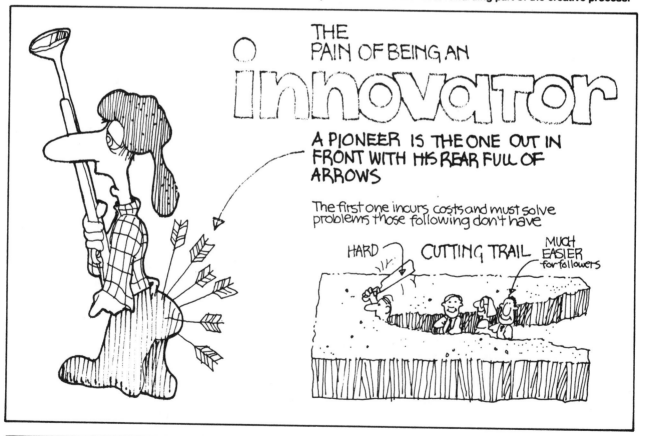

How to Achieve a Creative State of Mind

I've found a place that opens a person to a lot of creative ideas. It's a mental place, one we all share.

There are two mental approaches to creativity:

Either we work hard and long, expending a lot of effort—without assurance of return . . .

or we go to the place where ideas flow.

Either we go with the belief that hard, consistent effort is the best way to produce . . .

or we go to this place, where things flow soft and easy—yet produce!

What is this place I've discovered? Actually, the discovery didn't originate with me. Many creative people in the past have known about it:

> "I find that images appear only if we give our ideas uncontrolled freedom—when we are dreaming while awake. As soon as full consciousness, voluntary consciousness, returns, images weaken, darken; they seem to withdraw to some unknown region."
>
> Alfred Binet

When we're fully awake, we're able to work hard—but not necessarily creatively. When we're asleep, our minds flow, but we have no control over them. **The creative place is a place halfway between waking and sleeping.** That's where we can get the best results in our efforts to be creative.

The place has a name: **reverie.** For centuries famous creative people have talked about the creative power that's available through reverie. It diminishes the interference of the conscious mind and allows the subconscious to exercise its influence.

The result: enhanced creativity. The mind comes up with ideas and applications it would otherwise be blinded to.

Steps to Reverie

- **Prepare your mind.** To be able to enter the reverie state, the mind must be readied in advance. You need to eliminate stress and tension. You need to get rid of worries and strong emotions (such as anger or fear). Finally, you need to know what you want to get out of the reverie.

- **Find a place.** The physical location is important. It should be physically comfortable, but not so much so that you'll fall asleep. It should be removed from distractions: bright lights, street noises, ringing phones.

- **Relax.** Gradually relax both your body and your mind. One good way is to start with your feet and, as you inhale, feel the tension in your feet. As you exhale, imagine you're pushing the tension up through your body and out with your breath. Do the same thing with your calves, then thighs, and so on throughout your body.

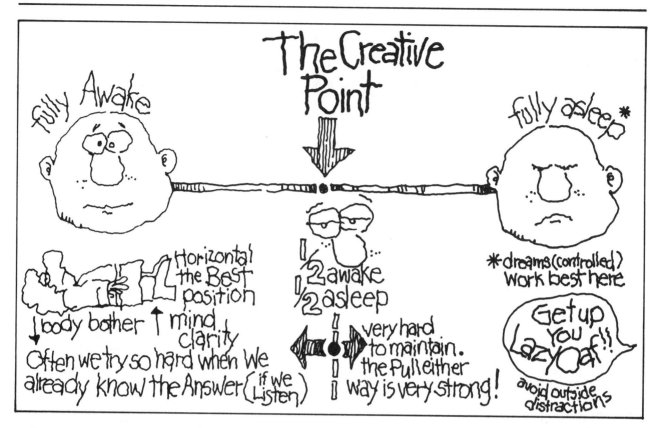

- **Hold yourself at the halfway place.** This is the hardest step. If you've been successful at relaxing yourself, it will probably be easy to go to sleep at this point. Resist the temptation and keep yourself in reverie, between waking and sleeping.

- **Ask the question.** When everything seems right, present your problem to the subconscious. It often helps to put it in the form of a question, or at least a clear and simple statement of the problem. Ask your subconscious for help, acting as if it's a separate, friendly entity—which it almost is! But don't try to overload your mind: one question per time, please!

- **Wait patiently for the ideas to come.** It takes a while for the mind to sift through its circuitry, especially if the problem is quite unique or difficult. Give it time to do its work.

If you can reach the point of reverie at will, you'll have taken a major step toward opening up the creative ideas that are too often locked inside.

Seedbed of Creative Thought

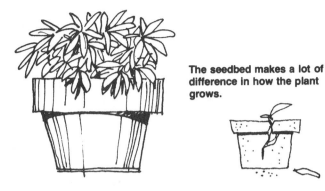

The seedbed makes a lot of difference in how the plant grows.

Take two identical plants and put them in pots. But have good soil in the first pot and poor soil in the second pot. Allow for good drainage in the first pot, but don't bother in the second pot.

What will happen? The answer is pretty obvious: the plant in the first pot will grow straight and strong. The second plant will languish and may even die.

They were the same plants in the same pots. But the seedbeds were different.

Often the best way to increase creativity is to modify the environment. If the creative ideas aren't coming, perhaps all you have to do is change your setting.

When I was teaching college students, they'd sometimes get stuck. They could try all they wanted, but the creativity just wouldn't come. That's when I'd change their environment—I'd move them into a different setting, giving them a different point of view. Their creative output would increase by 300 percent. And all I'd done was change the soil!

> "We should like to have some towering geniuses to reveal us to ourselves in colour and fire, but of course they would have to fit into the pattern of our society and be able to take orders from sound administrative types."
>
> J. B. Priestley

Gratefully, Priestley's dark view is only satirically correct. Creators still have the freedom to change environments—and thus to be creative.

Creating the Creative Environment

In looking for the administrative environment that will be most conducive to creativity, consider the following graph. The ideas apply to all settings: family, school, office, church, factory, and so forth.

The better the environment, the more creative a person can be.

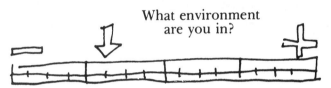

What environment are you in?

poor environment	good environment
invests in status quo	questions status quo
imposition from superiors	evolution from below
short-term view	long-term view
imposes direction	shared direction
intolerance of ambiguity	allows for fogginess
fear of losing	hopeful of gaining
desire to take control	gives freedom
emphasis on means	emphasis on ends
closed	open
regulates choices	trusts the decider
conventional approach	innovative approach
dominance of single value	has multiple values
reinforces the past	questions the present
quick to punish	long on patience
stays with the proven	will to take chances
won't take time	realizes it takes time
takes credit	gives recognition

It's About Time

Creative people as a group are often impatient. They'll painstakingly work their way through problems, covering all the bases, checking and double-checking. While they're in the process of creation they seem to be the models of patience.

Creations often take a good deal of time—sometimes years.

But then the creation is finished and ready to go. Suddenly that patient person is the height of impatience. Most creators find it hard to accept that it takes time to sell an idea. **It usually takes a good deal of time to bring an idea to fruition. Then one must add on the time it takes to take the idea to the public.**

Of course, some ideas are accepted immediately. Their time has come, and the public embraces them without a second thought. But others take much longer. Some ideas take only a matter of months to develop and sell. But those are the exceptions. A few examples of how long it can take to go from initial conception to final selling of an idea:

- Antibiotics—thirty years
- The zipper—thirty years
- Instant coffee—twenty-two years
- The ballpoint pen—seven years

Edgar Allan Poe submitted *The Raven* to more than forty publishers before it was finally printed.

Thomas Alva Edison had to go through more than 1,000 types of filaments before he finally found one that worked for his incandescent bulb.

Make Sure First

Before investing that kind of time, the creator needs to be very sure of himself. If he doesn't have a solid feeling, deep down inside, that the product or idea is one the public will want, perhaps he should reconsider.

"An important scientific innovation rarely makes its way by gradually winning over and converting its opponents: it rarely happens that Saul becomes Paul. What does happen is that its opponents gradually die out and that the growing generation is familiarized with the idea from the beginning."

Max Planck

Profit Others, Profit Yourself

MOTIVATION PRINCIPLE:

The more you give others what they want, the more they'll give you what you want.

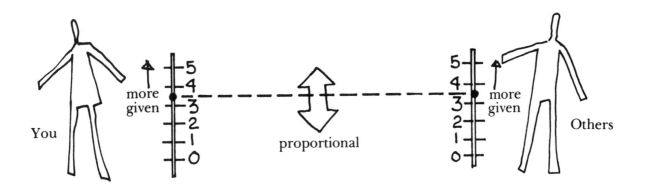

The true loner is a thing of the past. We live in a highly interdependent society, and those who find success usually do so with the assistance of others.

As you develop your creative idea, you'll soon reach the point where you need the help of others—either their time, their ideas, their energy, their money, or whatever. Here's a key that will help you get the most out of such relationships: **The more others can personally profit through helping you, the more they'll be willing to help.**

Tupperware, Shaklee, and Amway give us good examples of this principle. People who become involved in selling those products are personally benefited by their success. The more they sell, the greater their reward. The more people they can involve in helping them to sell, the greater their reward.

This same principle of rewarding people who help you is the approach that will help you find success. People are more than willing to help others if they are rewarded for their efforts.

Other Rewards Than Money

One caution: don't paint great pictures of wealth. If your prospective helper thinks you're making bundles of money, he'll expect bundles for his services. If you're typical, you're struggling to make everything work, including the finances. Make sure the people you entice into helping you realize that you aren't yet a wealthy person.

But there are other rewards than money. And, as a creator, you're in a unique position to offer such rewards. Everyone has dreams of wealth and fame. A ground-floor opportunity, which is what you have, gives people the vision of being in on something big. Appeal to people's egos, dreams, and other needs rather than offering money as a reward.

Here are some rewards you can offer:

- **Prestige.** People get great satisfaction in saying they are "developing a new product," or "working on a revolutionary new idea." You can even give them a title to gratify their desire for prestige.

- **New Experiences.** Just about everyone enjoys excitement in his life. And working on something that has big potential can be quite exciting.

- **Nice Guy.** Some people are just good at heart. They derive satisfaction from being nice guys. They would rather *feel good* about helping you than be paid for it.

- **Status.** It's not uncommon for people to drop names to show their importance. They believe you will think more of them if they can demonstrate that they rub shoulders with important people. These same people can use you to meet their need. They can say to their friends that they are "working on an exciting new invention," with "this guy who must be a genius."

- **Self-worth.** Some people will feel rewarded just for the opportunity to help you. They have always wanted to be creative. Working with you gives them the chance to see themselves as creative individuals working on an important project.

Be Sincere, Be Fair

The list of rewards could go on and on. The idea is to find out what motivates other people. Discover what they would most like as a reward, then try to offer it to them. The more the other person will profit by helping you, the more he'll help you.

But don't forget this key: Be sincere and fair in your dealings with others. Don't take advantage of anyone, or you may end up losing the advances you thought you'd make! As you seek to profit others, make it a genuine profit. Then everyone will benefit.

You've got to contact people to let them know what you have to offer before they'll ever be interested in helping you.

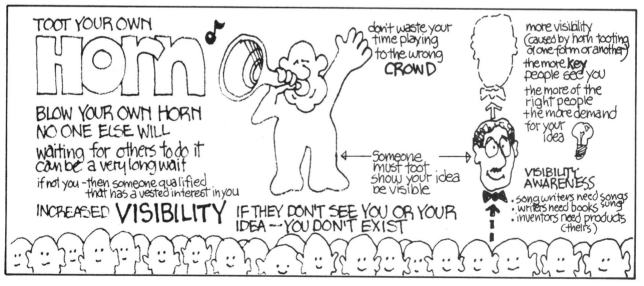

What Makes a Practical Idea?

In order for a creative idea to be financially successful, it must first be useful. As Thoreau said, "If you have built castles in the air . . . that is where they should be. Now put the foundations under them."

In other words, ideas in the head are fine. But it's much better to make them into something practical, something other people can use.

Who must see the idea as practical? The person who will be using it. A creation may have value to the creator, but it won't bring him any kind of financial reward until it also has value to the consumer. Even frivolous creations, such as the Pet Rock, must be seen to have some kind of value.

Some ideas may show evident genius, but they're totally unusable.

Jerry Haskell's family owned a huge cherry orchard. Every year Jerry was in charge of finding temporary labor to pick the cherries. When they ripened they had to be picked quickly, so that they didn't rot on the tree. Finding help was a real hassle, and every year Jerry dreaded harvest time.

Finally he decided to put his creativity to work to come up with a different solution. He was mechanically minded, and he began to create a cherry-picking machine. After an investment of much time and money, Jerry completed his invention. It was an elaborate, complicated, creative device. But when he tried to market it, he found that other growers preferred human labor to mechanical.

Now his cherry picker sits in the field rusting. It never sold and it's never been used. Jerry hadn't met the needs of the consumer when he created his invention, and all his work went to waste.

Idea Evaluation Checklist

Before you spend too much time and effort on a creation, ask how feasible it really is. How much value will others put on your creation? Here's a checklist to help you find out:

- *Is the idea a solution to a problem rather than just a definition of a problem?* Many creative thinkers define problems rather than solve them. They're great at pointing out what's wrong—but not so good at telling how to fix it. In determining the value of your idea, ask yourself: Can I describe the problem *as well as* the solution?

- *Does the idea fulfill a specific human need?* The need must be real—and your idea must be perceived by the buyer as fulfilling the need. Some of the needs people traditionally need filled are: (1) physiological needs such as food, shelter, rest, and exercise; (2) ego needs such as self-esteem, self-respect, confidence, independence, and education; (3) social needs such as belonging, friendship, and love; (4) safety needs such as protection against danger or threat or accident.

- *Do you know who will buy the idea?* It helps if you can describe the following: (1) where they live; (2) their buying habits; (3) a typical physical description, including age, sex, and so forth; (4) what they value in life.

- *Have you tested your idea on your intended buyer or user?*

- *What price does the consumer think the idea should sell for?*

- *Are you willing to sell the idea for the price the consumer is comfortable with?*

- *Do you know the channels of distribution for your product?* Where or how will the consumer buy your idea?

- *Is your idea an improvement over existing ideas?* Is it quieter, faster, safer, cheaper, easier to maintain, easier to use, more appealing, and so forth?

- *Does your idea work with related accessories already being used?* If it is a new tape recorder, for instance, does it use magnetic tapes such as cassettes or does it require completely new paraphernalia? A new recorder might not be difficult to market, but to change the whole recording market structure would be difficult.

In trying to determine what people want, look at yourself. What needs do YOU have that are unfulfilled?

New Eyes

"Every creative act involves . . . a new innocence of perception, liberated from the cataract of accepted belief."

Arthur Koestler

A young man graduated from the University of Utah with an engineering degree and was immediately hired by Kennecott Copper to help with their work in the mines. Kennecott owned a huge open-pit copper mine at Bingham, Utah, and the young engineer was assigned to figure out a more efficient way to align the railroad tracks used in hauling ore out of the pit. Since the pit was always changing in character, the network of tracks was also always changing.

It was an engineer's nightmare. And no one expected the new engineer to come up with any good ideas. The assignment was simply his initiation.

A few weeks later the young engineer came back with a detailed proposal. Rather than change the arrangement of the tracks, he said, Kennecott should use heavy trucks to haul the ore out of the pit. He showed his superiors figures to demonstrate that the trucks would save the company a significant amount of money.

No Preconceptions

Once he gave them the idea, everyone could see that it was self-evident. The plan was implemented and proved to be the very solution the company had always sought—but never expected to find.

Why had none of the other engineers seen that answer to the problem? The reason is simple: **We are all limited in what we see by what we expect to see.** The young engineer didn't share his colleagues' preconceptions, and thus he was able to think more creatively than they could.

Step Outside

Our culture, our environment, and our training all work together to create our expectations. To be successful in creativity, we need to step outside of those constraints and see things with new eyes.

- The cannon is a one-cylinder combustion engine. Leonardo da Vinci got the idea of adapting the cannon to create an engine for nonwar purposes. He put a piston into the cannon instead of a ball, but it wouldn't work effectively. In the following centuries, many inventors tried to get da Vinci's idea to work, but none had any success. Finally, in the nineteenth century, engineers looked at the whole problem with new eyes, replacing gunpowder with petroleum distillates. Their approach worked, and the internal combustion engine was born.

- When floods threaten in the United States and Europe, officials usually have the threatened area lined with sandbags. The bags effectively stop the water from leaving the desired course. But when the Japanese were faced with floods, they were unable to get enough sand to fill their bags. What were they to do? They looked at the problem with new eyes and came up with a different filler that works just as well, is much cheaper than sand, and is much more abundant. Instead of sandbags, the Japanese use . . . *waterbags!*

New eyes will give you waterbags instead of sandbags!

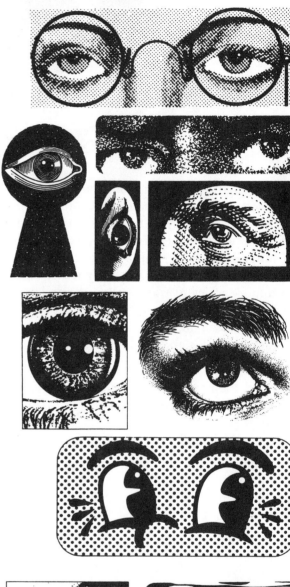

• A local supermarket once had a contest that awarded the winners a very special prize: three minutes in the store to pick up, free, everything they wanted. The contest had two winners. The first showed up at the time the prize was to be awarded, thinking she'd go from aisle to aisle

just as in her regular shopping. But the second looked at the problem with new eyes. She decided to go only to the areas that had the most expensive items. Accordingly, she spent several hours before the appointed time wandering around the store, making a master plan of how she'd collect her prize. It's easy to guess which of the women gained more value from the contest. Said Sir Henry Bessemer, inventor of a revolutionary process in steelmaking:

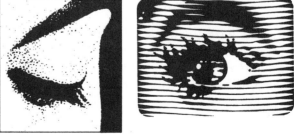

"I had an immense advantage over many others dealing with the problem inasmuch as I had no fixed ideas derived from long established practice to control and bias my mind, and did not suffer from the general belief that whatever is, is right."

Using the Mind's Eye

Through visualization, the image in the brain can become the reality in the hand.

"The pictures you create in your head often turn into the reality you hold in your hand."

Allan Hanson

One of the most vital of all creative approaches is to use the image in the mind to create something in reality. If a person can visualize something in his mind, he'll be able to experience it in his life—if he makes the effort to create the transition.

"Visualization enters into such disparate activities as painting, sculpture, choreography, architecture, astronautics, engineering, and photography. It is also helpful in playing baseball, moving furniture, and driving a car."

Richard de Mille

A few examples:

- Albert Einstein thought in images more often than he thought in words. He solved the problem of relativity through mental imaginings.

- Nikola Tesla invented the alternating current motor entirely in his head, working out the detailed plans mentally. Then he put it all down on paper. Tesla was apparently able to set up an invention in his head, turn it on, then return to it after three weeks to check it for wear!

- Tycoon Henry Kaiser claimed that he mentally saw the outcome of every one of his business ventures long before he achieved them in the external world.

- James Brindley, who engineered the English canal, would retire to his bed whenever he was faced with a particularly difficult problem. After working the problem out in his mind for two or three days, he'd have his solution, and would then arise and get to work.

- Oliver Evans, who invented the automated flour mill, also took to his bed. "I have in my bed viewed the whole operation with much mental anxiety," he said.

- Mozart composed entire scores inside his head. He said, "All this fires my soul, and, provided I am not disturbed, my subject enlarges itself, becomes methodized and defined, and the whole, though it be long, stands almost complete and finished in my mind, so that I can survey it, like a fine picture or a beautiful statue, at a glance. Nor do I hear in my imagination the parts successively, but I hear them, as it were, all at once. What a delight this is I cannot tell!"

"The art of archery is not an athletic ability mastered more or less through primarily physical practice, but rather a skill with its origin in mental exercise and with its object consisting in mentally hitting the mark.

"Therefore, the archer is basically aiming for himself. Through this, perhaps, he will succeed in hitting the target—his essential self."

E. Herrigel

"In oneself lies the whole world and if you know how to look and learn, then the door is there and the key is in your hand. Nobody on earth can give you either the key or the door to open, except yourself."

J. Krishnamurti

Steps for Visualization

Visualization comes naturally for many of us. But the effort can be enhanced, by anyone, by following these steps:

Visualization is simply watching an original movie in your mind, which can then be translated to reality.

1. **Reduce outside interference.** Find a place where you can be quiet and relaxed. Eliminate outside noise and concentrate on your internal processes. Close your eyes and look through your inner eye.

2. **Create a screen.** As you get images, project them on a movie screen in your mind. You can watch them almost as if you were an outsider.

3. **Evolve the image.** Move from the part you see initially to the whole there is to see, or from the whole to the part. Fill in the details. But don't force it—let the process flow naturally.

4. **Project the image into its context.** If you're working on a book, see your idea in the hands of the reader, and watch his reaction. If you're working on some kind of a device, mentally give it to a user, and watch what he does with it. If you're working on a technique, give it to someone who will apply it, and see how well it works. Mentally put the idea into its context, and test it out.

5. **Transfer the image.** This is the hardest step. Transfer what's in your head into reality. Show others the image. Create your internal view in an external form.

A Proven Aid to Creative Problem Solving

Picture the TV waves going through the air. What do they look like? What kind of motion do they follow?

If you're like most people, you'll have a hard time visualizing the waves that are sent out to televisions across the land.

Now visualize something else: picture those waves as they appear on your TV screen. Maybe see them in the form of your favorite nightly news.

Suddenly the waves become something *real*. One moment they were an ethereal nothingness floating through the air; the next moment they're a visible picture on your TV screen.

The same is true of ideas. While they're floating around in your head, it's hard for you to have a good grasp of them. But translate them into something real, something visible, and they take a meaningful shape.

The more real you can make your idea, the more successful you'll be in dealing with it. If you can convert it from *idea* to *reality* you'll be more able to create, develop, improve, and finally to sell it.

A New Kind of Sandwich

Stanley was an old inventor. At age sixty he invented, of all things, a new kind of sandwich. Every time he got a chance he'd tell others about his sandwich. "It's got this pocket in the bread, see, and you stick the ingredients inside." He'd gesture with his hands as he explained. "After the stuff is neatly packed in the pocket, you wrap the sandwich up, stick it in the freezer, and wait until you need it. Then you microwave it warm!"

Stanley's idea might have had some merit. But he didn't ever show anyone what the sandwich looked like, except with hand motions in the air. And, what's worse, he didn't ever make one for anyone to taste.

What kind of success do you suppose Stanley had in developing and selling his idea?

Edison Used a Model

At the other end of the spectrum is the example of Thomas Edison. He wisely made it a practice of always working in models. That helped him see how the invention looked and felt. It aided him as he worked out all the bugs. And when he wanted to show something to an investor or manufacturer, he had a prototype all ready.

When Edison got the idea for the phonograph, he gathered $15 worth of materials and used a foil cylinder to record and play "Mary Had a Little Lamb." He was amazed when his model actually worked—and on the first try! "I was never so taken back in my life," he said. "I was always afraid of things that worked the first time."

The DNA Model

Scientists tried for some time to understand the structure of DNA. They made models of what they thought it might look like, but their models never quite fit the data. One day James Watson was experimenting with a large model of the DNA molecule, shifting the different segments around in his hands. "Suddenly I became aware . . . that both pairs could be flip-flopped over and still have . . . bonds facing in the same direction." By working with a model, Watson and his colleagues were able to discover the double-helical structure of the DNA molecule. Their breakthrough resulted in a revolution in microbiology.

Ideas into Models

Creativity is heightened by converting ideas into models. The key is to convert the idea to something that can be experienced by the senses. Turn your idea into something that you can see, feel, taste, smell, or hear. Make a model of the idea. Only then will you be able to improve it, develop it, and sell it to someone else.

Here's a model of how the creative process may very well work.

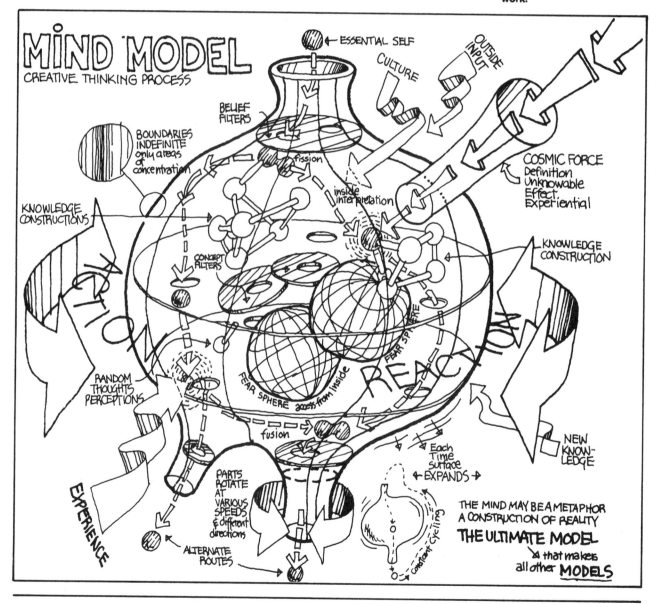

How to Win at the Creativity Game

When it comes to creative ideas, time is critical. The time between the inception of the idea and its translation into concrete reality should be as short as possible. Two reasons:

1. Speed is the best defense against getting ripped off by others; speed is the only way you can insure against the competition getting there first.

2. Some of the most important values one gets out of a creation come from others. Others can make you rich or famous. Or both. The sooner the idea becomes reality, the sooner those benefits will come.

Most races have two participants, a hare and a tortoise. It's a nice romantic idea to think the tortoise can win by being sure and steady, but if the hare will take off and keep up his speed, he'll win the idea race every time.

When Alexander Graham Bell was working on the telephone, another man, named Gray, was also trying to perfect the device. Both had their breakthrough at the same time. But Bell beat Gray to the patent office—by two hours. Neither man knew about the other, of course, but Bell became famous by being a little quicker. After all, who ever heard of the Gray Telephone System?

The creator of the Pet Rock also moved quickly. His idea was so simple it would be easy for someone else to rip it off. So he moved very carefully, getting trademarks and copyrights wherever he could. But he didn't trust such things to protect him. Instead he did all he could to promote his Pet Rock as fast as he could, getting all the customers and orders possible before the competition could step in.

Success Is in Your Own Hands

The key in promoting creative ideas is to recognize that your success or failure is in your own hands. A young man once captured a small bird and held it trembling in his hands. He took the bird to the wise old man of the mountain and held it behind his back. "This is my chance to show that the wise man isn't so wise after all," he thought. "I'll ask the wise man if the bird is alive or dead. If he says it is alive, I'll squeeze my hands and crush it to death. If he says it is dead, I'll let it fly away. Either way he'll be wrong."

Act Today

The young man stood before the wise old man of the mountain, holding the bird tightly in his hands. The villagers looked on. "Old man," the youth said, "I hold a bird in my hands. Tell us—is it alive or dead?"

The wise old man looked deep into the boy's eyes. He paused a long moment. Then he said in a low voice, "The answer, my boy," he said, "is up to you."

When it comes to making our ideas successful, our fate is in our own hands. But the faster we move, the more surely we move, the greater our potential will be.

Says Nolan Bushnell, founder of Atari, "The critical ingredient is getting off your rear end and doing something. It's as simple as that. A lot of people have ideas, but there are few who decide to do something about them now. Not tomorrow. Not next week. But today."

Credits

1. B.C. by permission of Johnny Hart and Field Enterprises, Inc.

2. *Funny Business* by Roger Bollen, reprinted by permission of Newspaper Enterprise Association.

3. Illustration by permission of Mike Richards, University of Utah graphics.

4. Carnival cartoon reprinted by permission of Newspaper Enterprise Association.

5. Becky Miller.

6. A collection and modification of checklists from *Applied Imagination* by Alex Osborn, *Conceptual Blockbusting* by James Adams, *The Universal Traveler* by Don Koberg and Jim Bagnall, and materials from The Creative Education Foundation of Buffalo, New York.

7. Illustration by permission of the Public Broadcasting Service.

8. Scott Bevan.

9. Mark Shultz, Kirk Henrichsen, Carl Haynie and Becky Miller.

10. Becky Miller.

11. Olinda Hoene.

Bibliography

"It's like people of similar thinking are just part of a great big living mind. They all share and help and build towards some distant goal they never fully understand, but are somehow obsessed with."

Design Yourself!, Kurt Hanks, Larry Belliston, Dave Edwards, Crisp Publications, Inc.

Rapid Viz, Kurt Hanks, Larry Belliston, Crisp Publications, Inc.

The Universal Traveler, Don Koberg and Jim Bagnall, Crisp Publications, Inc.

Put Your Mother on the Ceiling, Richard de Mille, Viking Press

Psycho—Cybernetics, Maxwell Maltz, Wilshire

Training Creative Thinking, Gary A. Davis, Holt, Rinehart and Winston, Inc.

Conceptual Blockbusting, James L. Adams, W.H. Freeman and Co.

Self—Renewal, John W. Gardner, Harper and Row

Design Methods, J.C. Jones, Wiley

The Metaphorical Way, William Gordon, Porpoise Books

Synectics, William Gordon, Harper and Row

Experiences in Visual Thinking, Robert McKim, Brooks/Cole Publishing Co.

On Knowing, Jerome Bruner, Belknap Press

Applied Imagination, Alex Osborn, Scribners

The Five-Day Course in Thinking, Edward de Bono, Pelican

New Think, Edward DeBono, Glencoe Press

The Psychology of Consciousness, Robert E. Ornstein, Viking

Cybernetic Creativity, Harold A. Rothbart, Robert Speller and Sons

The Act of Creation, A. Koestler, Macmillan

Pattern of Problem Solving, Moshe F. Rubinstein, Prentice—Hall, Inc.

The Art and Science of Creativity, George F. Kneller, Holt, Rinehart and Winston, Inc.

How to Solve Problems, Wayne A. Wickelgren, W.H. Freeman and Co.

Take the Road to Creativity and Get Off Your Dead End, David Campbell, Argus Communications

Index

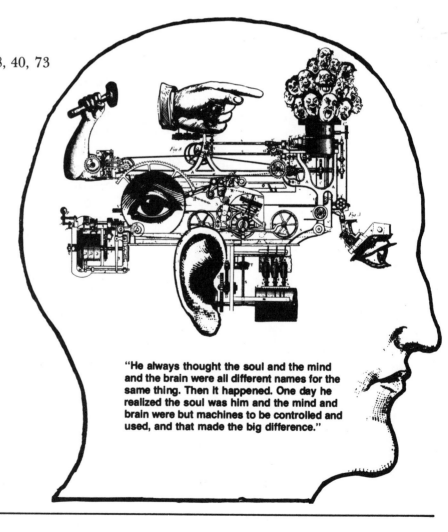

"He always thought the soul and the mind and the brain were all different names for the same thing. Then it happened. One day he realized the soul was him and the mind and brain were but machines to be controlled and used, and that made the big difference."